Grace and Justice on Death Row

The Race Against Time and Texas to Free an Innocent Man

BRIAN W. STOLARZ

FOREWORD BY SISTER HELEN PREJEAN

Skyhorse Publishing

Skyhorse Publishing books may be purchased in bulk at special discounts for sales promotion, corporate gifts, fund-raising, or educational purposes. Special editions can also be created to specifications. For details, contact the Special Sales Department, Skyhorse Publishing, 307 West 36th Street, 11th Floor, New York, NY 10018 or info@skyhorsepublishing.com.

Skyhorse® and Skyhorse Publishing® are registered trademarks of Skyhorse Publishing, Inc.®, a Delaware corporation.

Visit our website at www.skyhorsepublishing.com.

10 9 8 7 6 5 4 3 2

Library of Congress Cataloging-in-Publication Data is available on file.

Cover design by Rain Saukas
Cover photo credit iStock

ISBN: 978-1-5107-1510-3
Ebook ISBN: 978-1-5107-1512-7

Printed in the United States of America

Table of Contents

PART IV: THE FIGHT FOR DEWAYNE'S LIFE

PART V: JUSTICE, AT LAST

For Anna and the kids

For those who advocate to change the criminal justice system

For Dewayne

Foreword

It's almost a shame that Brian W. Stolarz decided to name his book *Grace and Justice on Death Row* because it's missing the word *Faith* in its title. And faith is the overriding fuel that fires this story. In many ways it's a story we've heard many times before. A police officer is murdered. A man, in this case Alfred Dewayne Brown, is accused of the crime, arrested, tried, convicted, and sentenced to death. In walks Brian, a young, brash lawyer, a devout Catholic, and a believer in offering his services pro bono to the indigent when he can.

The reason he agrees to take Dewayne's case is revealed in the book's opening:

> I knew Alfred Dewayne Brown was stone-cold innocent the moment I met him. He was a twenty-five-year-old, soft-spoken gentle giant with a sixty-nine IQ living in the Polunsky unit of the Texas Department of Criminal Justice in Livingston, Texas, north of Houston. Polunsky is where Texas houses people before it kills them.

Now think about that for a moment. You're introduced to someone you've never met before, and you can instantly determine whether he's innocent or guilty? That's not hope nor trust; that's faith, pure and simple.

Another word missing from the book's title is *perseverance*. As you'll read, the work Brian and his team performed took place over eight years. Perhaps more telling is that when a critical piece of evidence is revealed—almost by accident—it still takes a grinding two years to free Dewayne. What drives Brian to persevere? Why does he devote so much of his time to Dewayne's case when he also has a full-time job at a large law firm, as well as a young family to care for? His ability to examine and explain his feelings and motives while telling us the details of the case is what makes this book so compelling. Yes, the story of an innocent man on death row who is freed has been told before, but it's usually a dramatic recounting of conflicting evidence, or a story taken from the viewpoint of the accused. Rarely do we gain insight about what motivates his advocate and friend, the pro bono lawyer, and where they find their faith and perseverance.

Dewayne was just one of 263 prisoners currently on death row in Texas, one of 2,943 currently on death row in the United States. Brian, like me, is opposed to the death penalty and, like me, believes it will one day be rescinded, closing an open wound in the fabric of our society, even if it does leave an ugly scar. When you read *Grace and Justice on Death Row* and then realize how many other inmates have been exonerated from their accused crimes, I hope you'll agree we simply can no longer put to death those who may later be found innocent.

—Sister Helen Prejean, a Sister of St. Joseph, ministers to
prisoners on death row, author of *Dead Man Walking*

PART I:

Introduction

Chapter 1:

Brooklyn "BS Meter"

I knew Alfred Dewayne Brown was stone-cold innocent the moment I met him. He was a 25-year-old, soft-spoken gentle giant with a sixty-nine IQ living in the Polunsky Unit of the Texas Department of Criminal Justice in Livingston, Texas, north of Houston. Polunsky is where Texas houses people before it kills them. In 2005 he had been sentenced to die for the murder of a police officer, and he had been living on death row pretty much ever since. I was working for K&L Gates, a high-powered mega-firm in Washington, D.C., longing for a case I could be passionate about. I had worked for a couple of years as a public defender for the Legal Aid Society in Brooklyn, New York. It was a steady parade of fallible, devious, and occasionally innocent people, most of whom were short on money and shorter on luck. I felt something at Legal Aid—passion for my work.

In and out of the precinct houses, holding cells, and courtrooms I developed a more than functional "bullshit meter" about people accused of breaking the law. I can usually spot a lie or a liar better than a polygraph operator. I don't mean to brag, but just this one time I'll quote the late Muhammad Ali, who said, "It ain't bragging if you can back it up." I'm not bragging, I'm just saying after one look, I had absolutely no doubt—none—that Alfred Dewayne Brown had not committed the heinous crime for which he had been convicted and for which Texas was going to kill him.

When I left the Polunsky Unit an hour later, I promised Dewayne I would do my best to get him out of there. I also tried both to fight back tears and to keep from being sick to my stomach. I was grateful for the chance to save his life but scared it might be too late. The gravity of the situation set in instantly. I did not go to graduate school to save lives—that is what doctors do. But now I was given the opportunity to save one, and I was determined to do it. In fact, it became my legal, personal, and religious mission to do so.

But I could not ward off the thought that I might one day travel to Texas, stand behind a glass window, and watch a group of my fellow citizens carry out a medical procedure to end his life against his will. I was sick thinking I might have to watch. I vowed to my wife that if I watched him die I would hang up my law license forever and go start a pizza parlor. I am from New Jersey, after all.

I had a lot of work to do. At the Houston airport a few hours later, I was waiting for my flight, lost in thought about just how much work it would be, when I was accosted by a friendly, toothpick-wielding woman offering free samples of her cuisine around the food court. Unable to resist, I ordered and devoured some of her best General Tso's chicken. I cracked open my fortune cookie. "You love challenge," it said. I laughed and looked up to a ceiling painted with fake clouds. Was this some kind of divine-but-sick joke? I put the fortune in my wallet, where it remains to this day next to a picture of my three kids.

I know your initial reaction to all of this is to say, "Yeah, sure, all the people in prison say they are innocent." Hell, even members of my own family didn't believe me when I came home from Texas and said he was innocent. Believe me, I would be the first one to tell you if he were guilty. Many of my current and former clients were, in fact, guilty of what they were charged with. But, in that one moment, that first time I met him, something rocketed through to the deepest part of me: he didn't commit this crime. I understand your hesitation. Maybe you have your own BS meter. Come along with me on this ride and you, too, will see what I saw and felt, what I feel. This man is what I believed him to be from the very second I saw him—innocent. And he would have died if there were no one to stand up for him.

Chapter 2:

Against Scaliaism

"For me, one executed innocent man is too many."

As my fortune cookie said, I do indeed love a challenge, but I didn't know then what I know now—that Houston, Texas, is one of the worst, if not *the* worst, places in the United States of America to be charged with a crime. If you are African-American and poor, you might as well just get fitted for your none-too-stylish orange prison jumpsuit as you enter the courthouse, because prison is where you are going to be very soon. And for a long time.

And if you've been accused of killing somebody in Houston, you are headed for that sweepstakes of the damned known as the death penalty lottery. In the death penalty lottery, people convicted of capital crimes are chosen for execution by agents of the state who have their own personal and political agendas for seeking the death penalty.

As of the time this was written, 1,436 people have been executed in this country since 1976. However, according to Amnesty International, approximately *2 percent* of those convicted for crimes that are eligible for a death sentence actually receive a death sentence.

Now put yourself in Dewayne's shoes. He was an African-American man with limited intellectual functioning from a dirt-poor, marginalized family in Houston who didn't kill anybody, but was fingered by shady characters and the Houston Police Department for killing a white police officer in a very high-profile case. He was in a very dangerous place. He landed, without money or competent legal advice, in the death penalty lottery for something he didn't do.

The conviction of the innocent is less uncommon than the defenders of capital punishment care to admit. According to a 2014 study published by the *Proceedings of the National Academy of Sciences*, an estimated 4 percent of all inmates who have been scheduled to die are in fact innocent. And the authors stated that this figure was a conservative estimate. Some of the folks in the Texas death penalty abolition movement estimate that the number is much higher, even near 25 percent.

There have been 156 exonerations from death row since 1976, when the death penalty was reinstituted in America. Dewayne was number 154. Texas has had thirteen exonerees (Dewayne was lucky number thirteen) walk out of death row. They were sent to die and they walked out. When you analyze exonerations, including offenses beyond death row cases, a frightening portrait of Harris County emerges. According to the National Registry of Exonerations at the University of Michigan Law School and a *BBC Magazine* report, in 2015, there were 149 people exonerated from twenty-nine states after serving an average of fourteen and a half years in prison. Fifty-four were from Texas and a staggering forty-two of them came from Harris County. In 2014, there were 125 exonerations and Harris County had thirty-one of them (Texas had thirty-nine). And 52 percent of the Harris County exonerees were African-American, even though they make up less than 20 percent of the Harris County population.

Five hundred and thirty-seven people were executed by the state of Texas since 1976. According to the Death Penalty Information Center, an excellent resource for death penalty-related information, there is "strong evidence of innocence" for ten people who were executed; of those ten, six came from Texas. For example, it is without much debate now that Cameron Todd Willingham, who was convicted of setting fire to his own house while his three children were inside, was actually innocent and, thus, murdered by the state of Texas. There is also a strong indication that Troy Davis of Georgia was innocent, but he was executed.

I realize that ten out of 1,436 in the country and six out of 537 in Texas are small percentages, but we are talking about individual lives in each case and not numbers on a spreadsheet. Six people, or maybe more, may have been innocent, but the state of Texas killed them anyway. We will never know if they actually were innocent. They lay there on the gurneys with the drugs coursing through their veins, with the pain of a failed criminal justice system and country killing them. And even if they are posthumously exonerated, that obviously does not bring them back from the dead.

For me, one executed innocent man is too many.

So if you are a criminal defendant of any race who can't afford a good lawyer, and you are brought to justice in Houston, Texas, you may well wind up in line for a needle in your arm, containing a questionable drug cocktail that may cause you pain as you die. Pretty soon your mother will be crying over your pine-box casket as they lower your corpse into the soil of the Lone Star State.

But here is the catch, the dirty little secret that is no secret to anyone who works in the criminal justice system in Houston. You could also be innocent of a capital crime and looking at a doubly-damned fate: the end of your opportunity to prove your innocence in an American court of law and the simultaneous end of your life.

That's what Alfred Dewayne Brown and his family had been looking at for years when I met him in March 2007. Eight years and three months later, Dewayne would walk out of prison, giddy with the relief and joy we all felt.

"I went in an innocent man," he grinned on his first night of freedom in twelve years and sixty-two days, "and I came out an innocent man." And in a moment of pure grace and humility, Dewayne said that he had no hate in his heart about his time in jail, and he encouraged everyone to love each other and forgive.

It took a heroic effort from a small team of dedicated people, and some good old-fashioned luck (or the grace of God), to give Dewayne the last word in a story that might have been a terrible injustice.

I tell his story for a larger purpose: to show why the death penalty is dying in America. Dewayne's story is one of justice betrayed and justice vindicated, but it is only one of hundreds—if not thousands—of such cases, which have discredited our system of capital punishment as unfair and unfixable. As these cases accumulate, even those who do not reject the execution of criminals on moral grounds are rejecting the death penalty for practical reasons.

In 2015, conservative Nebraska (referendum vote scheduled for November 2016 after the Nebraska Legislature voted to abolish the death penalty) followed liberal Maryland as the latest state to abandon capital punishment. Nineteen states have abolished the death penalty. And in the states that still perform executions, the practice is receding. In 2012, just fifty-nine counties (fewer than 2 percent of counties in the country) accounted for *all* death sentences imposed nationwide. Since 1976, 82 percent of the executions in this country occurred in the south, and 37 percent of those in Texas. Only 1 percent of executions occurred in the Northeast.

In 1999, 70 percent of Americans lived in states that had carried out an execution in the past three years. In 2014, the figure was 33 percent. Executions have dropped dramatically since 2000, with only thirty-five in 2014, twenty-eight in 2015, and fourteen midway through 2016. In 1999, there were ninety-eight executions.

In other words, the places in America where capital punishment holds sway have been steadily shrinking. I will explain why the capital punishment system will almost certainly continue to contract until the day, not far off I believe, when it is no longer inflicted on the innocent or the guilty in America.

This is not a book about why the death penalty is unconstitutional (though I will explain why I think it is). It is not about why capital punishment is immoral (ditto). It is not a legal brief against an arbitrary process (because it is indisputable that the process is arbitrary). This is a book about why the death penalty is doomed for all of these reasons, and for several more.

My argument will no doubt strike some as premature, but I believe it is an argument whose time has come. The Supreme Court again upheld the practice of the death penalty in the *Glossip v. Gross* decision in June 2015. A group of prisoners on death row in Oklahoma appealed their death sentences, arguing the state's new method of execution—lethal injection of a drug cocktail using a sedative, not a barbiturate—would cause pain and thus violate the Eighth Amendment's injunction against cruel and unusual punishment.

"Because capital punishment is constitutional, there must be a constitutional means of carrying it out," wrote Justice Samuel Alito for the majority. "Challenges to lethal injection protocols test the boundaries of the authority and competency of federal courts," Alito went on. The courts, he opined, "should not embroil themselves in ongoing scientific controversies beyond their expertise."

The court's 5-4 decision preserved lethal injection as a constitutional way to kill Americans convicted of capital crimes. There are dozens of inmates scheduled to be killed for their crimes over the next three years, and there is no constitutional obstacle to their legally administered death. Texas executed two people in October 2015, and one in November 2015. Perhaps as a nod to the religious, Texas doesn't schedule any executions in December. The New Year brought four executions in January 2016, with more scheduled throughout the year.

What's more, the court's most prominent and arguably most influential jurist, former Supreme Court Justice Antonin Scalia, issued a separate concurring opinion. At this juncture I want to note that I wrote the majority of this book while Justice Scalia was still alive. When he died in February 2016, as a Catholic, I of course mourned his passing. I did not, however, mourn the fact that he is no longer serving on the Supreme Court, due to the part he played in damaging the same Constitution he is praised by most for defending, especially concerning the death penalty. It is not my intention to criticize someone who is deceased, but because many spoke of his legacy after his passing, I feel compelled to state that part of his legacy most likely contributed to the execution of innocent people in this country.

In *Glossip*, he scorned the arguments made by Justice Stephen Breyer in his dissent, wherein he claimed that the injustices inherent to the capital punishment system require its abolition in the name of American decency.

"Welcome to Groundhog Day." Scalia began with majestic, sarcastic scorn. "The scene is familiar: Petitioners, sentenced to die for the crimes they committed (including, in the case of one petitioner since put to death, raping and murdering an eleven-month-old baby), come before this Court asking us to nullify their sentences as 'cruel and unusual' under the Eighth Amendment."

The scope of Scalia's indignation elevated him so far above the practice of capital punishment in America that he could not—or did not want to—see what is actually happening in the jails, prisons, and courts of America. Four percent of the men and women on death row are innocent. Justice Scalia could not seem to acknowledge a story like Dewayne's. It would have distracted him from his lectures to a group of convicted criminals about their temerity to think the Constitution might apply to them. He even said that the Constitution does not preclude the execution of an innocent man. If he were alive to read this, he would likely dispatch of me and my words with another Scaliaism, as he did Justice Breyer in his *Glossip* decision. But he was wrong.

How dare the Oklahoma plaintiffs, men convicted of despicable and heinous crimes, assert their constitutional rights? How dare they ask for the protection of the Eighth Amendment?

"They rely on this provision because it is the only provision they *can* rely on," Scalia thundered on. "They were charged by a sovereign State with murder. They were afforded counsel and tried before a jury of their peers—tried twice, once to determine whether they were guilty and once to determine whether death was the appropriate sentence. They were duly convicted and sentenced. They were granted the right to appeal and to seek post-conviction relief, first in state and then in federal court. And now, acknowledging that their convictions are unassailable, they ask us for clemency, as though clemency were ours to give."

As I read Scalia's rant with mounting disbelief, I had to ask myself, "This man calls himself a Catholic?"

I grew up in circumstances not unlike Scalia: an extended Catholic family in the northeastern United States (Scalia in a multi-ethnic neighborhood of Queens in New York City, me in northern New Jersey). He attended a public elementary school and Catholic high school. So did I. He was self-described as "not a cool kid," who spent much of his time absorbed in his schoolwork. Same for me, until I grew taller than everyone else and figured out how to shoot a jumper on the basketball court. But I am a "law dork" at heart and, in truth, I love the law probably as much as Scalia did. That is why I am so upset about the criminal justice system in this country and why I believe Dewayne's story needs to be told.

PART II:

The Arrest

Chapter 3:

Two Senseless Murders

"Shit man, it's on."

After midnight and into the early morning of April 3, 2003, Elijah Joubert, Dashan Glaspie, and others were hanging out in the back alleys and in an apartment rented by Nikki Colar at the Villa Americana, a housing project in South Houston otherwise known as "the VA." They were shooting dice, drinking cough syrup laced with codeine, smoking blunts, and drinking a lot. The VA, needless to say, was not a veteran's hospital, and it was certainly not a villa.

The VA was a private apartment complex located at 5901 Solinsky Street with 258 units, all of which were subsidized housing for low-income people with residents paying very small amounts to live there. Dewayne's family lived there for a period of time and they paid twelve dollars a month for a two-bedroom apartment. The residents also called it "Dead End," a place where many went and never left. There were fistfights almost every night, along with occasional stabbings, and then a random spray of gunshots yielding a deadly fireworks display. Sex, drugs, and gambling comprised the VA's economy.

Dashan Glaspie, known as "Shon" or "P-Real," was a "jacker," a guy who robbed people. He did stick-ups at convenience stores and other small businesses around Houston, coming away with a fist of cash: five hundred bucks one time, fifty the next, depending on the drop when he was there. He sold weed. He had a tattoo on his arm that said "5901 Solinsky," the address of the VA.

Elijah Joubet's nickname was "Ghetto." He had arrests for possession with intent to distribute drugs, for carrying an unlicensed gun, and his biggest bid, four years, for an aggravated assault conviction. He had the same "5901 Solinsky" tattoo as Shon.

Around the VA, Shon and Ghetto were feared and respected.

So when Elijiah came up to Dashan and said it was on, Dashan said, "What's up, bitch? What's on?"

Shon said there was going to be a drop of $300,000 in cash at the ACE Cash Express store on the 610 South Loop in Houston. He had an inside connection who said she would help. It was to be a legendary score, one that would put them in the Ghetto Hall of Fame.

They got into the Grand Am, and Shon called his connection. "They just dropped it off," she said. "It's all there."

The $300,000 was in that store. And so the plan to jack the ACE Cash Express store in the morning took shape among them as they shot dice and drank. The inside connection said she would be opening the store in the morning. She wouldn't resist. They could get in and out with the money quick.

At five-thirty the next morning, Shon picked up Ghetto in his ratty white Pontiac Grand Am. Three of the four hubcaps were missing and dark-tinted windows only highlighted all the scratches on the body. A third man was in the passenger side, and this third man was key to the sorry story of how Dewayne almost lost his life.

In retelling the story, I've changed the name of the alleged third man because only a couple of people know he was there and they didn't snitch on him, leading the police and prosecutors to make a near-lethal case of mistaken identification. And I believe in not convicting someone when there hasn't been due process of law and that man is entitled to his own constitutional rights.

Ghetto told the third man to get out and get into the back so Ghetto could get into the passenger side of the car. It was too early for the ACE to be open, so they rode around for a while in south Houston. At about seven-thirty they drove to a gas station parking lot next to a different check-cashing store. They talked about robbing that store first. They were antsy. They were greedy. They were reckless.

They weren't counting on the shop owner, a white man named Leo Foisner, spotting them first. Foisner was talking to the first customer of the day when he saw the three men approaching. "This doesn't look very good," he told his customer. Foisner pulled out the pistol that he carried to and from work every day, and he displayed visibly at his side. He cocked the hammer as a warning. Shon, Ghetto, and the third man all saw the gun. They veered away without saying a word. They retreated back to the Grand Am, frustrated, but still ready to rob.

Shon went into the gas station and bought a strawberry soda, his favorite. As the three men loitered in the parking lot, two women passed by. They were sisters, LaTonya Hubbard and Natisha Price, and they knew Joubert and Glaspie from the VA.

"What y'all doing over here, Ghetto?" LaTonya asked Joubert.

"You don't know me," Ghetto said. "My name ain't Ghetto."

He said he was from Los Angeles, which was a lie to throw them off. He knew LaTonya and Natisha, but he wanted them to go away.

"Whatever," LaTonya scoffed. "We know you."

The two women paid for the gas and walked back to their car.

"Fuck, man, this ain't no good luck," Ghetto snapped as he got in the driver's seat. They drove back to the VA to plot their next move. They parked in front of an apartment where Shon's friend lived. Shon loaded a clip into his .45 caliber gun, which was modified with a laser sight. He loved the gun and took it everywhere he went, most of the time in a Nike Air Jordan shoebox. The third man had a .380 with a chrome handle. They had to work up some more bravado to get the job done.

"Are we gonna do this?"

"Yeah man, shit, let's do this shit."

"Three hundred, three hundred." They repeated the total so many times they could taste the score.

They headed to Houston's South Loop. They passed what seemed to be a never-ending string of strip malls with check-cashing places and payday lenders, no-name cell phone stores, Tex-Mex joints, and cut-rate gas stations. Just before nine o'clock in the morning they arrived at the ACE Cash Express store, which was in a small strip mall located next to a furniture store. They parked and waited in silence.

Ghetto, riding shotgun, didn't move. Shon was restless. He got out of the driver's seat. So did the third man in the back seat. They walked over to the furniture store, where Mohammed Afzal stood outside smoking a cigarette. A sixty-eight-year-old native of Pakistan, Afzal had opened the store that morning. One of the men asked Afzal a question about the price of some bedroom furniture. He answered, and they went into the store. Afzal stayed outside to finish his cigarette. Two or three minutes later the two men left the store.

Ghetto waited alone in his car. A woman pulled up in a red Pontiac Grand Am. She went up to the locked storefront and pulled out some keys. Her name was Alfredia Jones. She worked for ACE and it was her job to open the office. She was the mother of two children, a ten-year-old, and a newborn baby. In fact, she had just returned to work from maternity leave. Ghetto didn't know all that, but he did know she was *not* the woman Ghetto spoke with the night before. She was not the inside connection. What the hell was going on? Did she get cold feet?

Ghetto didn't give a shit. *It was on anyway.* He got out of the car. As Alfredia Jones unlocked the plate-glass door, Ghetto bum-rushed her into the store, let the door shut behind him and shoved her toward the back of the store. Shon and the other man saw Ghetto and followed him into the store.

Inside Ghetto was telling Alfredia what to do.

"Open the safe."

Alfredia said she had to notify the main office that the store was open or her bosses would suspect something was wrong. Ghetto warily let her handle the phone. Jones punched out the numbers. "Opening store twenty-four," she said, and hung up. Ghetto had no idea that "store twenty-four" was the company's code for a "robbery in progress."

Alfredia put the phone down.

"Open the safe."

The other men entered the office.

"Why y'all doing this?" Alfredia asked. "Why y'all robbing us?"

Within five minutes, Houston Police Officer Charles Clark arrived at the mall on the South Loop. He was a twenty-year honorable veteran of the Houston Police Department who had exactly one day left before he was eligible for retirement. He parked his patrol car and hastened toward the storefront. He could see two men inside. He spoke into his microphone, calling for backup.

"Step it up," he said. "They have guns."

Officer Clark entered the unlocked door, gun drawn. The door opened into a passageway, called a man-cage, with a second door into the office. Officer Clark opened the second door and fired at one of the men inside. The bullet missed both, exploding into the office wall. One of the men shot at him and a bullet grazed his shoulder. Officer Clark tried to shoot again. Silence. His gun, an old model Browning semi-automatic, jammed. One of the men fired again. The bullet hit the highest point of Officer Clark's forehead, just within the hairline. He fell to the ground, dead already. When he came to rest, his foot was propping the front door to the store open.

Shon grabbed Alfredia from behind. He pressed the gun down on her right temple.

"Why y'all doing this?" she was still saying.

Ghetto looked to Shon. He had finally figured out what "store twenty-four" meant.

"P, this bitch played us."

Alfredia Jones was shot and killed. Ghetto would be convicted of her murder.

Shon, Ghetto, and the third man ran out of the store to the car. The white Grand Am pulled out into traffic, leaving behind two dead people. The crime took seven minutes to commit. The men obtained no money. No three hundred grand. Instead of a legendary ghetto score, they were looking at a murder rap and the needle.

Three people were responsible: Ghetto, Shon, and a third man. The third man was the one who shot Officer Clark in a senseless, stupid act of cold-blooded murder. The state of Texas believed the third man was Dewayne and was ready to kill him for it. But it wasn't Dewayne with Ghetto and Shon that day.

The three men went back to the VA and split up. Ghetto told Shon that he planned to lay low, and he should do the same. Ghetto's girlfriend came to get him and they left. Ghetto called the third man and asked him what he was doing. He said he was hiding out at his house, that he might go to school to try to create an alibi.

Unlike Elijah Joubert and Dashan Glaspie, he succeeded in creating that alibi. And Dewayne Brown took the fall. The third man's plan almost worked.

Chapter 4:

Manhunt

Truck driver and police scanner hobbyist James Wheat was listening to the Houston Police Department radio channel on the morning of April 3, 2003, like he always did. When he heard the call about a robbery at ACE Cash Express, he drove straight to the scene. He was pulling into the parking lot, about fifty feet away from the storefront, when he saw Officer Clark responding to the call. He heard Officer Clark call for backup. He heard gunshots. He saw Officer Clark fall. He saw three black men running out of the store. Wheat later recalled that two "dark-skinned black males about five-seven to five-eight got into the front seat of the vehicle." A third, taller black male got into the back of the white Grand Am, he said.

Wheat ran toward Officer Clark as the men fled. He took one look and knew it was too late. He used Clark's radio to call for help.

Soon the TV stations were reporting a shooting incident at a check-cashing office in South Houston. "Police are looking for three men in a white older model Grand Am," went the reports. When LaTonya Hubbard and Natisha Price heard that, they called the police straightaway. They had seen Shon and Ghetto hanging out in a white Grand Am that morning at the gas station, and they were acting funny. They told the police they should be looking for Glaspie and Joubert. Who knew? There might be reward if they helped the police catch the men who killed the lady and the police officer.

LaTonya and Natisha went to the crime scene to try to talk with police but they couldn't get through to anyone, so they went back to the VA. Eventually some Houston policemen found them there. They listened to their story and began canvassing the VA, trying to gather information from the people who would talk with them.

Various names were mentioned—not only Shon and Ghetto, but also names like "Deuce," "Little Red," "Smooth," and "Ju-Ju." The police talked to a man named Lamarcus Colar, brother of Nikki Colar, whose apartment the men were hanging out in the night before. Lamarcus mentioned Shon and Ghetto, and he also mentioned "Doby," a.k.a. Alfred Dewayne Brown. He said that he thought he saw him in his sister's apartment. He didn't actually see him, but that wasn't a story that many people cared to hear—the police had their three suspects and were closing in and closing in fast. They wanted to resolve this case as quickly as possible. They wanted justice.

Chapter 5:

Family and Faith and Growth

"For it is in giving that we receive."

My father taught me my work ethic and to have passion for your work. He put on his tool belt every day and ground out a living for our family as a union carpenter. He ran a side business that turned into a full-time endeavor. I worked for him in the summer and he treated me the same as everyone else, demanding hard work. He hustled and worked harder than anyone else and made money on his projects, even the most difficult ones. He could make a "dollar out of fifteen cents," one of his workers told me. "But don't let him catch you loafing," they also said.

My grandfather, a huge influence in my life, worked on the production line at Continental Can, a can factory in Paterson, New Jersey, and my grandmother was a school nurse for the same school, P.S. 24 in Paterson, New Jersey, for over fifty years.

Our family drove American cars. My father drove only Ford vans. My grandfather drove an Oldsmobile and always talked about owning a Cadillac one day when he won the lottery. My mother drove a Chevrolet Chevette with plastic seats that stuck to your legs in the summer. We thought we were high society when my father's business started doing well and we bought an ice-blue Chrysler New Yorker with a Landau roof that had one of those electronic voice things that would say "a door is ajar" when a door was open. We spent summers on the Jersey shore at Cape May and Wildwood Crest, where I later worked as a lifeguard at a boardwalk water park.

We spent a lot of time with my family that was scattered about northern New Jersey, usually convening at my grandparents' two-family home on Madison Avenue in Paterson. Sunday dinner was a big event, with spaghetti or chicken cutlets on the menu. Never fancy, but always good.

There was nothing lavish or extravagant about my childhood. A trip to get a hot dog at my favorite places (Rutt's Hut and Hot Grill) or to a pizza parlor for a slice was exciting for me. When I was in middle school my mother bought me one of those black Michael Jackson jackets with all the zippers and pockets—I thought that it was the coolest possession I ever had.

I loved collecting baseball cards and was (still am) obsessed with the New York Mets. I watched every game of the 1986 season; the play when Mookie Wilson's ground ball went through Bill Buckner's legs was the best sports moment of my life. I shot hoops in our driveway for hours. I walked down to the corner deli, Otto's, and bought a pack of baseball cards for a quarter, and maybe a bottle of birch beer if I had enough money.

And we went to church. A lot. I basically lived at my grandparents' church, Blessed Sacrament in Paterson, New Jersey. If I sat through mass with my grandmother and behaved myself and said all the responsorial psalms correctly, I got one dollar. My grandparents' house had religious artifacts all over the place, with a huge Virgin Mary statue in the backyard, and a large poster of Jesus over their bed. We went to bingo nights, tricky trays, fish frys, community service projects, and many special events at the church. I was too young to fully realize it, but that parish formed my religious foundation.

Once during the decade-long effort to exonerate Dewayne, I left the prison where he was being held. A church group was passing out bibles to the public and fish platters to the prison staff. The prison staff was "Doing God's Work," proclaimed a banner draped over a table.

I asked if I could have a fish platter. They asked me if I was a prison guard. I said I was a defense attorney for one of the men on death row. They looked at me like I was Satan himself and pushed the fish platters back away from my hand. Instead of a platter, they handed me a bible. One woman recommended I read it to my client before he went to the Lord.

I didn't want to say what I was thinking: that a benevolent and just God would probably not be cool with the execution of an innocent man, or anyone for that matter. I wished I had the right biblical passage I could throw back at her but I didn't. I wish I had said that an eye for an eye makes everyone blind and that I believed in the Jesus who told us to turn the other cheek and love each other and seek redemption and forgiveness, and in Saint Francis who taught me that it is in pardoning that we are pardoned. I just took the bible and said thank you. That night I read some Psalms and some New Testament passages in my hotel room, and I went to sleep thinking about Dewayne (as I often do) and (as I also often do) my religious upbringing.

I loved growing up in the Catholic Church, first at my grandparents' church and then my family's church, St. Mary's, a Franciscan parish in Pompton Lakes, New Jersey. At St. Mary's, I met the men who shaped my spiritual life, Father Michael Carnevale and Father Kevin Downey. They taught me about life, love, tolerance, and how to serve others. When I got married many years later, Father Mike came to Dallas to officiate my wedding. He delivered a thoughtful sermon about love and perseverance, saying that "love is the fruit of the struggle," and then, because he was a wiseass like me, he turned to the crowd and said, "I now present Mr. and Mrs. Anna Stolarz."

Growing up in a Franciscan parish had a huge impact on who I became and what I value in life. The parish took the foundation I had from my grandparents' church and formed my Christian spirit. I felt alive every time I was on the grounds of my church.

Saint Francis of Assisi is my favorite saint for his dedication to serving the poor. We have a sign in our home that is an excerpt from the Prayer of Saint Francis that says, simply, "for it is in giving that we receive." And I make sure my kids try to live their lives that way in their daily actions and in church service projects.

Before we had kids, Anna and I went to Italy for two weeks and made sure that we stopped in Assisi just to see and feel the holy ground where he lived. And, of course, it is very cool that Pope Francis chose his name after Saint Francis. I was fortunate to get a ticket to the Papal Mass at Catholic University in September 2015, and I was five feet away from him when he processed in.

My time at Catholic University Law School in Washington, D.C., in the 1990s clarified and solidified my desire to continue my religious mission to serve others while using my skills as a lawyer. It was why I became a public defender in Brooklyn, why I always did pro bono work when I was in private practice at the law firm of K&L Gates, and why I do pro bono work today. And I will always do it.

I received an award in 2007 for taking the most pro bono cases for indigent people from the Catholic Charities Legal Network, a division of Catholic Charities for the Archdiocese of Washington that places cases for needy individuals with volunteer lawyers. In 2014, I received the Caritas award from Catholic Charities, the highest service award the organization gives in service to the poor. And I am very fortunate to have Catholic Charities for the Archdiocese of Washington as a trusted client. Father John Enzler is the CEO, and he is one of those unique, wonderful shepherds who is focused on service to the poor and needy and says that, when it comes to service, "Say yes every time you can and no only when you have to."

But I didn't, and don't, do pro bono work for awards or recognition. I just think it is a duty of any lawyer to give their talents back to those who can't afford a lawyer. It's that simple to me. It is the perfect confluence of my legal training and my religious upbringing. And it makes me feel alive inside every time I do it. Pope Francis said that "we all have the duty to do good," and my duty was to Dewayne. That duty was why I stayed with his case until I hugged him in 2015, why I love him like a member of my own family today, and why I thank God every chance I get that he is out of prison.

What any of us think about the death penalty in America is shaped by a combination of hard facts, deeply held beliefs, and complex emotions and thoughts about the biggest questions in life—justice, public safety, and human nature.

In America, we tend to want someone to take on the bad guys who do bad things without mercy. From our cinematic mythology of the Hollywood western to the modern TV detective shows, Americans like stories about bringing the bad guys to justice. Appeals to "get tough on crime" have often proven popular in political American elections. Elected judges in Texas (more on them later) don't get re-elected if they are seen as "soft on crime." We all remember Willie Horton, don't we? I can still see his face from those political ads, the image of the turnstile spinning to let him out, and I was scared of him.

At the same time, Americans pride themselves on a legal and constitutional system with built-in, strong safeguards for the rights of individuals. English legal scholar William Blackstone said that it is better to have ten guilty men go free than to have one innocent suffer. And Thurgood Marshall gave a speech where he preferred a thousand guilty men going free rather than ten innocents suffering!

But even the politician I idolized growing up, Bill Clinton, signed into law one of the toughest bills on crime in our recent history, the Violent Crime Control and Law Enforcement Act of 1994. Three-strikes laws and serious mandatory minimums for federal drug offenses were instituted and copied across state penal systems. More federal inmates were put in prison during his terms than those of Presidents George H.W. Bush and Reagan combined. Clinton also signed the Antiterrorism and Effective Death Penalty Act of 1996, which limited the habeas corpus relief of federal inmates. All of this was, in fact, "tough on crime," and expedient politically, but at what fiscal and personal cost?

I read recently that President Clinton feels remorse about the impact of those laws. He should. But remorse doesn't help the folks who served and lost all that time. Don't get me wrong, people should be punished for crimes they commit, but there has to be a way to modulate how and for how long we imprison people, to give serious consideration to alternative drug courts for those with substance abuse issues and mental health courts for those with mental health issues. Give individualized sentences for individual crimes, not stiff mandatory minimums that stash people in prison for years. President Obama is trying to rectify the policies of the past by issuing 562 commutations for low-level drug offenders who received long sentences due to mandatory minimums. These commutations are more than the nine prior Presidents combined. This is an excellent start but there are many more who need to be considered for sentence reductions and more will hopefully be issued by the end of President Obama's term.

Of course, the lens of race shapes how we understand crime and justice. Camera cell phones, police body cameras, and social media are documenting racialized police practices unknown to many whites. I was exposed to it during my time as a public defender. I was also exposed to it by Chuck D and Public Enemy, who told me to "Fight the Power" in 1989. I won the cassette on the Wildwood boardwalk and played it so much it broke.

The movie the song came from, *Do the Right Thing*, changed my life. When I was young, we moved from the rough streets of Paterson to the quaint, serene, lower-middle-class town of Bloomingdale, New Jersey. I was pretty sheltered and not exposed on a daily basis to racial issues. The only people who didn't look or talk like us were the nice German family who ran the deli down the street from my house.

The issues from the movie are still the issues of our time and I get depressed when I see that things don't seem to have changed that much. We may not have expected the vigiliance of a movement such as Black Lives Matter to be so necessary still, in our time. But the disparity in how blacks and whites are treated by law enforcement and the criminal justice system is obvious, and it needs to change. Today's racism is not as out in the open as it used to be (even though it took a senseless and terrible hate crime to finally bring the Confederate flag down in South Carolina). This racism is present every day in the criminal justice system and is statistically significant in its outcomes. The majority of death row inmates are executed for killing white victims, while African-Americans make up a majority of the homicide victims in this country. Similarly, researchers in Virginia found that a person is three times as likely to be sentenced to death for murdering a white victim than a black victim. One in three African-American men will spend time in prison during their lives, according to a 2013 study by the Sentencing Project, a Washington, D.C.-based group that advocates for prison reform. You've heard these stats so often you get numb to them, but you shouldn't.

They are a nationwide embarrassment. This pervasive racism almost led to the public execution of an innocent, intellectually disabled African-American man.

The lens of class also affects how we think about the death penalty. When was the last time a rich man was executed in America? Leopold and Loeb were charged with capital murder but spared the death penalty, thanks to well-paid Clarence Darrow. Texas oilman and multi-millionaire T. Cullen Davis was acquitted due to prominent defense attorney Richard "Racehorse" Haynes. "The death penalty is for poor people," said Stephen Bright, director of the Southern Center for Human Rights in Atlanta. At one point in the early 1990s, every single member of death row in California was eligible for court-appointed counsel. Every one. If you can afford a decent lawyer, you are very unlikely to be executed, no matter how heinous your crime. If you can't afford one, it could kill you.

A second and equally important issue of our time is inequality in this country. Inequality is real, getting worse by the day, and the death row housing units across this country are housing the poor and preparing to execute them, oftentimes without the constitutional guarantees our country proudly claims to extend to all citizens. Pope Francis is welcomed wherever he goes, not because he's dining with the powerful and the rich, but ministering to and commiserating with the poor. It is time we all followed that lead.

The point is that seemingly huge and immutable truths about American thinking can change. The social consensus that allowed Jim Crow segregation laws and banned interracial marriage held firm for almost a hundred years after the Civil War. And then it collapsed in the 1960s. Attitudes about gay marriage and drug prohibition have undergone a sea change in recent years. The same is happening with capital punishment. When people see the ugly face of death penalty justice close up, and then Dewayne's face, they start to have second thoughts.

Dewayne's is such a case that it has caused even the staunchest of my death penalty supporter friends to take a second look. All I ask is that you are open to take that second look, too.

Chapter 6:

Interrogations

Houston Police Department officers swarmed though garden apartment complexes and cordoned off cheap motels known for criminal activity, looking for the white Grand Am. It didn't take long. A police SWAT team assembled, barged into the motel room, and arrested Dashan Glaspie.

Shon was taken to an interrogation room. He gave a long sequence of ever-changing stories. He was in a motel with his girlfriend on the day of the incident. He said he had sex with her from six to eight in the morning. Then he went to the VA around ten to sell some marijuana to his regular customers.

Try again, the detectives suggested. One of them played the good cop, the Zen cop. "I want to believe you. I'm not saying you shot the officer, all right, but I know you were with Doby [meaning Dewayne] and you were with them and you were at that place when this happened."

He urged Shon to help himself, to say what happened.

"You don't hurt people, Shon, that's not your nature, that's not your character. . . . Shon, just let it out. Shon. Let your soul come into alignment with your body because you are in such conflict. Shon, I can assure you that people will honor the fact that somebody takes responsibility for what happens."

Shon changed his story. He said Ghetto and Doby told him they wanted to rob a dope dealer, and that they just needed Shon to drop them off near the ACE store and pick them up. Shon claimed he dropped them off behind the ACE store. A few minutes later, he said, Doby and Ghetto came running to the car, and Shon took them back to the VA.

The detectives didn't buy that version either. They told him he wasn't going anywhere until he started making sense. Shon cried, and he lied.

"I ain't got no guts to shoot nobody, man, I can't do that. I dropped them off by the ACE store."

This wasted several hours.

The cops told Shon that witnesses had described someone fitting his appearance at the crime scene.

"Do the honorable thing, Shon, admit to what you did, speak from the heart and let your heart flow. We're throwing you a lifeline, man, you either reach for it and you swim, or you sink."

Shon tried again. He said that he was in the ACE with Dewayne and Ghetto. He said that he was in the back area by the safe to look for cameras and panic buttons. He then said he ducked down so the police officer couldn't see him. He denied that he shot anyone:

"I just ducked behind the thing, they start going towards the door or whatever, I didn't see neither one of them get shot and that's the honest truth. I didn't see the lady getting shot or the police officer. The police officer was on the ground and she was in there."

He said Dewayne was in the front of the store while he was in the back. He never said that he actually saw Dewayne shoot Officer Clark.

Chapter 7:

"What y'all want me to say?"

Ghetto was picked up by police based on the identifications from LaTonya and Natisha. He was put into an interrogation room at the Houston Police Department next to the room where Shon was spinning his tales. Ghetto "appeared to enjoy the attention he was getting," one policeman observed. He came off as a "street-wise criminal" who "talks freely of being good at making other drug dealers go hungry and have to get on a new block."

Ghetto said that Shon sold drugs and robbed people for a living and he always carried his favorite .45 handgun. He also said that Shon threatened him, and told him that if he were to talk to the police about the incident, he was going do something to his family.

"I ain't shoot nobody, I didn't have no gun."

The detectives informed Elijah they were going to go to his mother's house and his grandmother's house to "find shit and lock them up." Knowing what all was stored at his mother's house, this was not something Ghetto wanted to happen. The detectives said Shon had already made a statement and impli-cated him. He was going to take all the heat if he did not make a statement. It was time, because time was running out. According to Ghetto, the detectives also got physical with him during the interrogation, hitting him multiple times.

"What y'all want me to say?"

"I want you to say that Brown shot the cop," one of the policemen said. "Shon shot the woman. I'll see if I can help you."

"You're not going to fuck with my family?"

"You got my word on that."

With that, Ghetto told them what they wanted: Shon shot Alfredia Jones, and Dewayne shot Officer Clark, took him down with one shot. Shon shot Ms. Jones point-blank a moment later.

"It all happened so quick," he began.

After Ghetto finished giving his statement, he remained in a holding cell in the Houston Police Department before being transported to the Harris County Jail.

Chapter 8:

Dewayne's Alibi

"He said he never left Ericka's house."

The phone began to ring and ring again at Ericka Dockery's house. She and Dewayne were dating, and he lived at her house. People were saying they heard Dewayne was involved in the shootings at the check-cashing store. Dewayne could not believe it. He decided to go to the police station to tell them he did not do anything like that. On his way there, a police officer spotted him and pulled his car over. Dewayne was arrested.

During the subsequent interrogation, Dewayne denied any involvement. He said he last saw Ghetto and Shon the night before at the VA. He spent the night at his girlfriend's house and stayed there through the morning after she went to work.

According to police reports, Dewayne cried when he was interrogated. He was frustrated but never confessed to any involvement. He would "stare and glare" under questioning, the report said. He "showed no emotion." He "refused to listen."

One detective wrote that he had "tried to get him to acknowledge that he had at least been seen earlier on Thursday with Ghetto and Shawn [Shon]. I told him several times that things can get out of control. He hung his head, wiped his eyes and said he understood everything I told him and that things can get out of control but he last saw Shawn and Ghetto on Thursday night. He said he never left Ericka's house."

The police did not believe Dewayne. They put him in a lineup for various witnesses to come forward and try to make a positive identification.

James Wheat did not recognize anyone in the lineup.

Natisha Price, who saw Ghetto, Shon, and the third man in the gas station parking lot, did not recognize anyone in the lineup.

Latonya Hubbard recognized Dewayne, but not from the day of the incident. She knew him from the VA.

Mohammed Afzal, the furniture store employee, said he was not certain but said that he may be 80 to 85 percent certain that Dewayne was the man who asked him the question outside the store.

Another furniture store employee identified a different person in the lineup as the person they saw at the crime scene.

Leo Foisner, owner of the first check-cashing business approached by the three men that day, said that Dewayne "looked familiar," but he could not make a positive identification.

None of the eyewitness identifications at the lineup were very strong.

The Houston Police Department detectives were undeterred. From the start, they focused on Dewayne as the third man who had been seen at the site of two murders. When Shon said Dewayne was involved, they believed him.

There was only one problem: Shon lied. He didn't want to be a snitch on the third man who was there. So he let the blame fall on Dewayne, who went to the police to clear his name and never left.

Chapter 9:

"Doing Justice" at the DA's Office

"It is so important for prosecutors to play fair, not just to win."

The Harris County District Attorney's Office took the initial information from the police to conduct its investigation. The assigned district attorney was a veteran homicide prosecutor, Daniel J. Rizzo, a very successful prosecutor with more than twenty years of experience in capital cases. Many a man on death row in Texas can thank DA Rizzo for putting him there.

The Harris County District Attorney's Office was also home to the "Silver Needle Society," the name given by former District Attorney Johnny B. Holmes, Jr., to the death penalty unit in the office, and purportedly a sign proudly listed all the inmates who were executed from the County. "Death by Injection" is the name of a rock band comprised of Harris County DAs. Harris County, Texas, lives by a hardcore, eye-for-an-eye frontier justice mindset. Mess with them, and you end up in the ground.

The first thing Rizzo did was to try to strike a deal with Dashan Glaspie. He needed to get a cooperating witness, or snitch, to make his case. He made an offer to Shon that was nearly impossible to turn down: a thirty-year sentence to a lesser charge of aggravated robbery. All he had to do was testify against Ghetto and Dewayne. These types of deals are how many criminal cases unfold—find the guy willing to "rat out" his co-defendants, and the others usually fold after that or get convicted at trial.

For a defendant deeply implicated in a murder case, it was a sweet deal. In Texas, as in most states, offenders can be eligible for parole after a period of time in prison, especially if the person is well behaved while he serves time. Typically, the offender has to serve about half of the sentence. Shon could be out in fifteen years. He accepted the offer, pleading guilty to aggravated robbery, and agreed to testify.

With Shon locked up, Rizzo had his sights set on the other two perpetrators. But he had a legal hurdle to overcome. In Texas, there is an "accomplice corroboration rule." This means that when prosecutors have a case involving a cooperating witness, like Shon, who has an obvious motivation to implicate others and assist the state's case to get a more lenient sentence, the prosecutors have to present independent corroborating evidence to prove the case. Even in Texas, the state can't make a case against someone based solely on self-interested cooperating witnesses.

Rizzo knew that he didn't have a forensic case against Dewayne. Based on the preliminary police investigation, there were no surveillance videos from the ACE offices or surrounding businesses, no DNA or blood evidence at the scene, no fingerprints, no gunshot residue on anyone's hands. There was no CSI-type evidence to use. Rizzo had to focus on getting eyewitnesses to corroborate Shon's story that Dewayne had shot Officer Clark.

One of the ways Rizzo conducted his investigation was to use the grand jury process. A grand jury is a group of people from Harris County who sit in a room, typically the size of a school classroom, and listen to evidence presented by the district attorney. The DA's job is to present sufficient evidence to secure what is called a "true bill," or an indictment against the defendant. The grand jurors themselves can also ask questions, and they often do.

The grand jury process is not open to the public. There is no judge moderating the proceeding. There is only the district attorney, a court reporter, a bailiff or marshal, and, of course, the witness who is called to testify. Grand jurors are required to attend for weeks or even months at a time, so they become familiar with each other and also familiar with the prosecutor. In short, a grand jury proceeding is nothing like a jury trial.

While I was a public defender in New York, I was permitted to be in the grand jury room to watch if my client testified, but that is rare among criminal justice systems. I was also able to suggest witnesses to the prosecutor to present to the grand jury. In most states, and in federal court, defense attorneys are relegated to sitting outside the grand jury room. When my clients testified before a grand jury, I read outdated copies of *Sports Illustrated* and *Newsweek*. I also did a lot of my favorite word game, Jumble. And I sat worried about how my client was being treated. I always told them to come out and talk with me whenever they had a question, and even though their security blanket was sitting right outside, very few clients ever came out to talk with me. They answered the questions, and then we would go to a coffee shop to debrief and de-stress.

It is safe to say that if a prosecutor wants an indictment against someone, he or she will get one. "A grand jury would 'indict a ham sandwich,' if that's what you wanted," New York State Chief Judge Sol Wachtler once said, a quote made famous by novelist Tom Wolfe in *The Bonfire of the Vanities*. That line has been repeated by countless criminal defense attorneys talking to clients who wonder, "Will I get indicted?" In this case, Rizzo used the grand jury like his own personal deli to turn Dewayne Brown into an indictable ham sandwich.

He almost got away with it—but he didn't. And his failure illuminates a second reason the death penalty is dying: pervasive prosecutorial misconduct.

In the American system of justice, prosecutors have immense power: the power to decide what charges to bring. "Since 97 percent of cases are resolved without trial," the editors of *The New York Times* observed in a 2014 editorial, "those decisions are almost always the most important factor in the outcome. That is why it is so important for prosecutors to play fair, not just to win." This obligation, embodied in the Supreme Court's 1963 decision in *Brady v. Maryland*, requires prosecutors to provide defendants with any exculpatory evidence that could affect a verdict or sentence.

The continuing failure of prosecutors to heed their *Brady* obligations is fueling a judicial backlash. As federal appellate judge Alex Kozinski, appointed by President Ronald Reagan, declared in a 2013 decision, "There is an epidemic of *Brady* violations abroad in the land. Only judges can put a stop to it." And as judges act on Kozinski's call, they will inevitably undermine Judge Scalia's claim that capital punishment in America is fairly applied and justly administered.

The evidence supporting Judge Kozinski is everywhere. In 2009, a federal judge dismissed the ethics conviction of former Senator Ted Stevens of Alaska with a harsh condemnation of the prosecutor's conduct. In his decision, Judge Emmet G. Sullivan, a personal hero of mine, declared that in his nearly twenty-five years on the bench, he had "never seen mishandling and misconduct like what I have seen" in the Stevens case. Sullivan, appointed by President Bill Clinton, warned about a "troubling tendency" of prosecutors to stretch the boundaries of legal ethics and to conceal evidence for the sake of winning cases. He took the extraordinary step of appointing a special prosecutor to investigate the Justice Department lawyers who oversaw the prosecution of Stevens. The special prosecutor who examined the botched prosecution issued a report that said he found evidence of willful concealment of information from Stevens's defense lawyers. The evidence would have aided in Stevens's defense. The report was particularly critical of two prosecutors but did not state that they committed any criminal offenses themselves. Defense attorney Brendan Sullivan said it was "the worst misconduct we've seen in a generation by prosecutors at the Department of Justice."

The effects of prosecutorial misconduct were not deadly in Stevens's case, but they were certainly consequential. Days after Stevens was convicted on seven felony counts in October 2008, he was defeated in a bid to win a seventh term. He had been the longest serving Republican in the history of the Senate. In a statement, Stevens said that the prosecutor's behavior had "nearly destroyed my faith" in the American judicial system. "Their conduct had consequences for me that they will never realize and can never be reversed." If Stevens had been charged with a capital offense, he might not have lived to utter those words.

As prosecutorial misconduct damages people's faith in the American judicial system, it inevitably undermines support for the death penalty as well. In 2013, the investigative news site *ProPublica* identified thirty state and federal court rulings in which judges explicitly concluded New York City prosecutors had committed "harmful misconduct" that was sufficient to throw out convictions, several of them in capital cases. More than half of the cases involved *Brady* violations, according to *ProPublica*.

In ten of the cases, defendants who were convicted at least in part because of prosecutorial abuse were ultimately exonerated, often after years in prison. Jabbar Collins served fifteen years for a murder he didn't commit. The district attorney's office acknowledged that it withheld exculpatory evidence. Collins filed a $150 million lawsuit against the city and settled the case for $10 million. Shih-Wei Su, arrested at age nineteen, was incarcerated for twelve years on attempted murder charges before a federal appeals court ruled that a prosecutor had "knowingly elicited false testimony" to win a conviction. The city eventually paid Su $3.5 million.

In the case that provoked Judge Kozinski's ire, federal prosecutors seeking to convict Kenneth Olsen of developing a biological agent for use as a weapon did not disclose the results of an investigation about a forensic scientist who testified at his trial. The prosecutors relied on the scientist's testimony knowing that a group of experts questioned his "diligence and care in the laboratory, his understanding of the scientific principles about which he testified in court, and his credibility on the witness stand." The prosecutors merely told Olsen's lawyers there were "purely administrative" complaints about DNA testing, which was not used in Olsen's case. Olsen was convicted.

"When a public official behaves with such casual disregard for his constitutional obligations and the rights of the accused, it erodes the public's trust in our justice system and chips away at the foundational premises of the rule of law," Judge Kozinski wrote.

"A robust and rigorously enforced *Brady* rule is imperative because all the incentives prosecutors confront encourage them not to discover or disclose exculpatory evidence," Kozinski said. "Due to the nature of a *Brady* violation, it's highly unlikely wrongdoing will ever come to light in the first place. This creates a serious moral hazard for those prosecutors who are more interested in winning a conviction than serving justice."

Did Dan Rizzo have a "serious moral hazard" in this high-profile case? Did he want a conviction more than justice?

Chapter 10:

Pressuring the Witnesses

"Next time it's going to be the cops and the Child Protective Services coming to take your children."

The most critical witness Rizzo called to testify before the grand jury was Ericka Dockery. Prior to his arrest, Dewayne lived with Dockery and her three daughters, ages ten, seven, and five. Dockery's two cousins, Reginald Jones and Ruben Jones, also lived with her.

On April 21, 2003, Dockery testified to the grand jury that at the time of the incident, she worked for a home healthcare company at a client's home from 9:00 a.m. to 1:00 p.m., Monday thru Friday. She also worked at Subway from 4:00 p.m. to 10:00 p.m. most nights. On the night before the incident, she and Dewayne fought. She told him he had to move out of her house. Normally they slept together in her bedroom upstairs, but that night Dewayne slept downstairs on the couch. Dockery got up at 6:00 a.m. and went downstairs. She saw Dewayne on the couch, and she saw either Ruben or Reginald playing a video game. She tapped Dewayne on the shoulder and said, "Didn't I tell you to get out of my house?" He rolled over, looked at her, laughed, and rolled over to go back to sleep. She said, "I'm not even going to start with you this morning." She went on with her morning and got her kids ready for school.

At about 6:45 a.m., she walked her kids to the bus stop. Dewayne continued to sleep on the couch. Dockery came back from the bus stop, and Dewayne was still there. She testified that Dewayne was still there on the couch, asleep, at 8:30 a.m. when she left for work.

Dockery left her home and went to work at the home of Alma Berry, an elderly woman Dockery was taking care of. She got to Ms. Berry's home right before 9:00 a.m. She called home at about 9:30 a.m., and talked with her cousin Reginald. She asked Reginald if Dewayne was still there. He said that Dewayne got up from the couch and went upstairs to continue sleeping.

After 10:00 a.m., Dewayne called her at Ms. Berry's house. Ms. Berry's caller ID indicated that he was calling from Dockery's house. When the call came in, Ms. Berry looked at the caller ID and said, "Ericka, it's your house."

Dockery testified that Dewayne said that they needed to talk "about us." He asked if she had seen the news. He told her to watch Channel 26. Dockery knew it was around 10:00 a.m. because Ms. Berry liked to watch "The Price is Right" and "Ricki Lake," and they were on during that time. She saw the news about a shooting at ACE Cash Express store.

"That's where—ain't that where you go cash your check at?" Dewayne asked. "You think it's that girl who be in there that got shot?"

Dockery left Ms. Berry's house at 1:00 p.m. and went home. Dewayne was there when she got home. He said he was feeling sick. They took a nap together before Dockery went to work at Subway.

Dockery's cousin Reginald Jones, who was eighteen at the time, testified to the grand jury that he and his brothers Ruben and Richard were at Dockery's house on the night of April 2, 2003. Reginald saw Dewayne and Dockery argue that night. The next morning, Reginald said he got up around 9:30 or 10:00. He saw the murders reported on television. Then he saw Dewayne *come downstairs* from Ericka's upstairs bedroom. Reginald explained that he was sitting on the couch, which enabled him to see both the front door and the back door of the apartment. In other words, Dewayne could not have come into the house earlier and gone upstairs without Reginald seeing him.

Reginald's testimony was consistent with a statement he gave to the police on April 4, 2003, the day after the incident. In that statement, he said that on April 3, 2003, he woke up "around 9:30 or 10:00 a.m. and went downstairs and started playing video games. No one else was up yet." Reginald stated that he saw Dewayne came downstairs later in the morning.

"I know he came from upstairs because when I am sitting on the couch in the living room I can see who comes in the front door and who comes in the back door. There's a mirror right in front of you when you're on the couch so you can see who is coming downstairs, too."

Dockery and Jones provided a very strong alibi for Dewayne.

Rizzo proceeded against Dewayne anyway. He did not investigate the alibi to see if it was legitimate or open the investigation up to include other suspects. Well, he did do something to investigate the alibi, but more on that later.

Instead, he badgered and threatened Ericka Dockery to change her testimony to fit his case.

First, Rizzo offered Dockery an "opportunity" to change her testimony to avoid what he said was going to be severe perjury charges. Rizzo specifically wanted her to change her statement that Dewayne was on the couch when she left at 8:30 that morning. Rizzo asked if she wanted to change her testimony in any way. She said that the time could have been different, but Dewayne was there when she left for work.

Dockery was reminded of the consequences if she lied and did not change her story. One grand juror told her she seemed like a "good, nice young lady," and "a hard-working young lady," adding that "if we find out that you're not telling the truth, we're coming after you."

> GRAND JUROR: And if we find out that you were lying, under oath, you can be in serious trouble.
> THE WITNESS: I understand.
> GRAND JUROR: And you won't be able to get a job flipping burgers.
> THE WITNESS: (laughing) Yes, sir.
> GRAND JUROR: You got three children that you're trying to take care of . . .

Dockery was told she would not have another opportunity once she left the room. "Who's going to take care of your three kids?" she was asked. "Nobody."

Dockery persisted. She said that between 6:00 a.m. and 8:30 a.m., Dewayne was at her house, sleeping on the couch.

Dockery speculated that she may have left earlier and gone to get some breakfast first before going to Ms. Berry's house. Pressed on this point, she said she just did not remember the exact time.

When asked if she could have left before 7:30 a.m., the approximate time when Leo Foisner saw three men approaching him, Dockery said it could not have been because Ms. Berry would not have let her in the house that early. Her shift started at 9:00 a.m.

In the grand jury room, Rizzo continued to press Dockery to admit to an earlier departure time. She simply could not push the time any earlier than 7:30 a.m. She stated that she got back from taking the kids to the bus stop at 7:00 a.m., and then she had to get dressed for work after that. She said she was just not sure of the time.

One grand juror advised her that her kids would need "some parental guidance in the future." She said she needed to look out for herself.

"You know by working in the home healthcare, and there's a felony charge brung [sic] against you, you know that's over with."

The exchange continued:

> THE WITNESS: I know. Everything is over.
> GRAND JUROR: You won't be able to go get a decent job anywhere.
> THE WITNESS: Nowhere. I already know.
> GRAND JUROR: And it's not worth hiding behind no man.
> THE WITNESS: Oh, it's not. It's not. I can always get another man, but I could never get another life.
> GRAND JUROR: Nor is your children [sic]. That's why [Mr. Rizzo] is constantly asking you if there's anything you want to change before you leave.
> THE WITNESS: You know, maybe I'm misunderstanding the question. But I'm trying to answer the best way I can.
> GRAND JUROR: It's so important. Because he's not worth it.
> THE WITNESS: Okay. No, he's not . . .

The foreperson of the grand jury then asked Rizzo about the punishment for perjury, using his first name:

> FOREPERSON: Hey, Dan. What are the punishments for Perjury and Aggravated Perjury?
> MR. DAN RIZZO: It's up to ten years in prison.
> FOREPERSON: In prison. Okay.
> GRAND JUROR: Oh, no.
> THE WITNESS: You know I'm just—I'm just trying to answer all your questions to the best of my ability.

A grand juror is supposed to be an impartial person that decides whether the district attorney has enough evidence to indict someone. The grand juror in this room was talking to Rizzo like a friend. My wife was a prosecutor and she worked with many grand juries. She says no one has ever called her by her first name in the grand jury. And in all the times I have sat in to watch a client testify, no grand jury ever showed that level of familiarity. It troubled me the first time I read it.

And to set the record straight, it is highly unlikely that anyone would go to prison for ten years for perjury. What Rizzo did was state the statutory maximum for a perjury conviction, which is hardly ever given, especially not to individuals with little or no criminal record such as Dockery. This was just a scare tactic floated by Rizzo, and he had the supposedly impartial foreperson on his side. They were ganging up on her, and it was working.

Rizzo then told Dockery that there were two people who saw Dewayne at the VA at 7:00 a.m. that day. Despite all this, Dockery continued to testify that when she left that morning, he was on the couch.

Ericka was threatened yet again.

> FOREPERSON: . . . Like we said, and if you are—the evidence shows that you are perjuring yourself then you know the kids are going to be taken by Child Protective Services, and you're going to the penitentiary and you won't see your kids for a long time.

Another grand juror said, "[N]ext time it's going to be the cops and the Child Protective Services coming to take your children."

One of the grand jurors said, "[G]irl, you just a big mistake." Dockery tried to back off her statement that Dewayne was there when she left for work, with grand jurors repeatedly telling her, "[T]hink about your kids."

> GRAND JUROR: One minute, Erica. He wasn't in the house when you put your kids on the bus, either, was he?
> THE WITNESS: I'm trying to remember.
> GRAND JUROR: Think about your kids, darling.
> THE WITNESS: I'm trying to remember.
> FOREPERSON: That's what we're concerned about here, is your kids.
> GRAND JUROR: He was not at the house—
> FOREPERSON: We're as much concerned about your kids as you are. So, tell the truth.
> GRAND JUROR: He was not in the house when you put your kids on the bus, was he? Tell the truth, girl.
> THE WITNESS: **Yes, he was there.**

As her testimony closed without Rizzo getting precisely what he wanted out of her, Rizzo told her that he thought she was involved:

RIZZO: I think—what I think it is, I think that you're up to your neck involved in this deal. . . {End excerpt}

Rizzo was very unhappy with Dockery's testimony. He needed her to say that when she left for work, Dewayne was not there. He was so unhappy that he wielded the only power he had left—he charged Dockery with three counts of perjury. He didn't believe her, so he charged her, simple as that.

The charging document Rizzo filed against Dockery alleged that she lied when she said that she last saw Dewayne at 8:30 a.m. on the day of the incident when she actually last saw him at 6:50 a.m., a time that was very convenient for Rizzo's case. He charged her because he could, because he wanted to cool her out in jail. He wanted to exert pressure over her, make her feel insecure and vulnerable. He needed her testimony badly.

When Dockery was brought to court for her arraignment on the perjury charge, Rizzo requested a high bail, $5,000 for each count. Bail requests are often based on risk of flight (meaning the defendant would flee upon release and not come back to court), or danger to the community based on some violence in the person's past, or the charge was a violent one. Ericka did not have a criminal record, maintained a residence in Houston, and worked two jobs to support her three children. She was no danger to the community and unlikely to flee. That didn't matter—Rizzo wanted her in jail, or else his plan wouldn't work. And besides, Ericka did not have the scratch to post bail.

When I was a public defender, I was assigned to night arraignments, as seen in the old TV show *Night Court*. As the individuals were arrested, charged, and brought before a judge for the first time, I made dozens of bail arguments per night. There is a 99.9 percent chance that Dockery would have been released on her "own recognizance," or promise to return, or a very nominal bail set if Rizzo didn't act the way he did. Rizzo later bragged in his opening statement in Dewayne's trial that he purposefully asked for a high bail for Dockery, because he knew she would not be able to make the bail and she would have to sit and stew in jail. This is one of the worst parts of this case, because it reflected the district attorney's ability and power to manipulate witnesses, particularly an indigent African-American woman, and get exactly what he wanted.

And it worked. Dockery remained in jail for *four months*. She had to rely on her sister to take care of her three small children, and was concerned they might be sent to a foster home. She went to the grand jury and told the truth as she saw it. For her trouble, she was taken away from her kids for 120 long days. The pressure in this case was immense for Dockery, and she simply could not stand to be in prison any longer.

In January 2004, nine months after the incident and five months after Dockery was incarcerated, she changed her story. She provided a statement that Rizzo could finally use against Dewayne. Dockery's new story was that she saw Dewayne on the couch during the early morning of the incident, but when she returned from taking her children to school at 7:25 a.m., apparently Dewayne was no longer there.

Dockery said she then went to work to take care of Ms. Berry and got there by 8:30 a.m., even though she continued to say she didn't enter Ms. Berry's house until nine o'clock. At ten, the phone rang and Ms. Berry said, "It's your house," after looking at the caller ID. Even though Dockery recalled this very specific statement by Berry regarding the caller ID information, she said in her new statement that Dewayne had called from "Shondo's," the home of a woman who lived at the VA. Later in the day of the incident, Dockery said she confronted Dewayne about the allegations that he was involved in the shootings, and he denied it.

Dockery then stated that she went to visit Dewayne at the Harris County Jail after he was arrested for the case and he "steady denied it over and over." He said "he wasn't there, he don't know nothing and Ghetto and Shawn [Shon] were lying on him."

Dockery claimed that she visited Dewayne every day until mid-July 2004, when he instructed her to lie to the grand jury and say that he was home on the morning of the incident. She further claimed that she spoke with Dewayne's brother, A.B., about the incident, and that he had told her that Dewayne was involved. When she next spoke to Dewayne, she said he said, "I was there, I was there."

Dockery was released from jail. She had to wear an ankle bracelet that monitored her whereabouts everywhere she went. She had to take a drug test twice a month. She also had to call a homicide detective once a week to talk about the case and go over her testimony. But she was out and back with her kids, which was all she cared about, even with all the conditions.

Rizzo had his star witness and corroboration for the version of Shon's ever-changing story that suited his purposes. It was time to go after Dewayne.

Chapter 11:

Indictment

"I will not sign for something I didn't do."

Rizzo believed that he had what he needed to convict Dewayne and sought an indictment against him. On July 25, 2005, the Harris County Grand Jury indicted Dewayne in Cause No. 11035159 for the capital murder of Officer Charles Clark. The indictment alleged that on or about April 3, 2003, Dewayne, "while in the course of committing and attempting to commit the robbery of A. Jones, intentionally caused the death of C. Clark by shooting C. Clark with a deadly weapon, to-wit, a firearm." Because it was a capital murder charge, the most severe penalty for the crime was the death penalty. Rizzo also charged Elijah Joubert with the capital murder of Alfredia Jones.

The case was assigned to Judge Mark Kent Ellis, a former Harris County District Attorney and part-time religious minister. Ellis was an elected judge and ran as a Republican.

Dewayne was brought to court to be formally presented with the charge. He pled not guilty and received two court-appointed attorneys because he could not afford his own counsel. The attorneys appointed to Dewayne's case were Loretta Johnson Muldrow and Robert Morrow. In Harris County death penalty cases, defendants who cannot afford counsel are appointed two attorneys from a list of attorneys who are approved to take death penalty cases based on their prior experience. Typically one attorney handles the trial or "guilt/innocence phase," and one handles the sentencing, or "punishment phase." In this case, Muldrow was the trial counsel, and Morrow was the sentencing counsel.

Prior to trial, Dewayne was offered a plea deal of forty years in prison, an extremely reasonable plea offer for a person who allegedly murdered a police officer. Almost too reasonable—it telegraphed some weakness in the state's case. He would have been eligible for parole in twenty years. Muldrow and Morrow, and other death penalty attorneys in Houston who were not formally working on Dewayne's case, tried to convince Dewayne to take the deal and cut his losses and avoid being convicted and sent to death row. This was a sweetheart deal, they kept telling him. You will not go to death row and you can be out in twenty years. You have to take it, they would tell him. They don't give these kinds of deals in cop-killing cases. They pleaded with him. Dewayne refused the deal every single time. He said he was innocent, and he said it again and again. "I will not sign for something I didn't do," he said. At one point, Muldrow said that if she were in his shoes, she would take the deal. "Then you take it and do the time," Dewayne said. "I didn't do this crime."

It was time for trial.

PART III:

The Trial

Chapter 12:

Gideon Betrayed

"The law is a system that protects everyone who can afford a lawyer."

On June 3, 1961, someone broke into the Bay Harbor Pool Room in Panama City, Florida, smashed a cigarette machine, and stole money from a cash register. Later that day, a witness reported that he had seen a man named Clarence Earl Gideon leaving the pool room with a wine bottle and money in his pockets. Based on this accusation alone, the police arrested Gideon and charged him with breaking and entering with intent to commit petit larceny.

When Gideon appeared in court the judge said, "Mr. Gideon, I am sorry, but I cannot appoint counsel to represent you in this case. Under the laws of the State of Florida, the only time the court can appoint counsel to represent a defendant is when that person is charged with a capital offense. I am sorry, but I will have to deny your request to appoint counsel to defend you in this case."

"The United States Supreme Court says I am entitled to be represented by counsel," Gideon protested. The court declined to appoint counsel and Gideon had to act as his own attorney. He argued his innocence to no avail. The jury returned a guilty verdict and Gideon was sentenced to serve five years in the state prison. From his prison cell, Gideon appealed to the United States Supreme Court in a suit against the Secretary of the Florida Department of Corrections. And so the United States Supreme Court in 1963 addressed a basic constitutional question: does the Sixth Amendment's right to counsel in criminal cases extend to felony defendants in state courts?

Yes, the Court said unanimously in March 1963. In delivering the opinion of the 9-0 majority, Justice Hugo L. Black held that the framers of the Constitution placed a high value on the right of the accused to have the means to put up a proper defense, and the state as well as federal courts must respect that right. The Court held that it was consistent with the Constitution to require state courts to appoint attorneys for defendants who could not afford to retain counsel on their own.

Justice William O. Douglas wrote a concurring opinion in which he argued that the Fourteenth Amendment does not apply a watered-down version of the Bill of Rights to the states. In a separate concurring opinion, Justice Tom C. Clark wrote that the Constitution guarantees the right to counsel as a protection of due process, and there is no reason to apply that protection in certain cases but not others. Justice John M. Harlan wrote a separate concurring opinion in which he argued that the majority's decision represented an extension of earlier precedent that established the existence of a serious criminal charge to be a "special circumstance" that requires the appointment of counsel.

Thanks to the court's decision, Gideon was granted another trial. He demonstrated that the testimony used to convict him was fallacious and he went free. It was a landmark of American justice.

As United States Attorney General Robert F. Kennedy remarked at the time, "If an obscure Florida convict named Clarence Earl Gideon had not sat down in prison with a pencil and paper to write a letter to the Supreme Court, and if the Supreme Court had not taken the trouble to look at the merits in that one crude petition among all the bundles of mail it must receive every day, the vast machinery of American law would have gone on functioning undisturbed. But Gideon did write that letter; the court did look into his case; he was re-tried with the help of competent defense counsel, found not guilty, and released from prison after two years of punishment for a crime he did not commit. And the whole course of legal history has been changed." A replica of good old Earl's handwritten petition to the Supreme Court and a picture of him are in my office. And *Gideon's Trumpet*, the book written about the case, is on my mantle.

The *Gideon* decision paved the way for the public defender system now in place in all fifty states. Every American charged with a felony has a right to counsel. Millions of Americans have had their constitutional rights protected as a result. Yet the fact remains that the reality of the right to counsel is often elusive and often violates the same rights Mr. Gideon sought.

Fifty years later, another United States Attorney General, Eric Holder, speaking at a Department of Justice event celebrating the *Gideon* decision, acknowledged that "despite half a century of process—even today, in 2013, far too many Americans struggle to gain access to the legal assistance they need. . . . In short, America's indigent defense system exists in a state of crisis." Holder went on to declare it was "time to reclaim Gideon's petition—and resolve to confront the obstacles facing indigent defense providers."

The *National Law Journal* cited numerous examples about the dire state of indigent defense on the fiftieth anniversary of *Gideon*. The state of Wisconsin pays its private lawyers forty dollars an hour to represent indigent defendants, and that rate has not changed since 1978. In Louisville, Kentucky, public defenders are assigned nearly five hundred cases a year and are paid a miserable $38,770 a year. The most I ever had as a public defender in New York was about one hundred cases, which was pretty hard to handle, and I was paid $60,000. I cannot imagine what it would be like to handle five hundred cases for far less. With five hundred cases, the *National Law Journal* article noted, all an attorney could do was "meet 'em and plead 'em."

The article noted the systemic problem: that "it's politically popular to pay the salaries of the police and prosecutors," but much less so to fund indigent defense. I saw an example of that firsthand. When the congressionally mandated across-the-board budget sequester hit the federal government in 2013, friends of mine who worked for the Federal Public Defender in D.C. and Maryland had "furlough Fridays" and were not paid for fifteen or even twenty days. They also had to cut lawyer positions, investigators, and support staff. One public defender said that the cuts didn't cut close to the bone; they cut the bone. A friend told me she essentially had to take a month without pay, which really hurt her family's finances. But, she said, the attorneys in her office still went to work because they couldn't just give up a day of work for their clients. What stung the most, though, was that the Department of Justice lawyers did not face any furlough days and they actually hired new prosecutors. So the lawyers who were trying to put folks in jail were getting paid in full, and the ones who defend the rights of the accused were forced to take unpaid holidays. Justice Sonia Sotomayor, a former prosecutor herself, noted in a recent Supreme Court opinion that, "in the end, states are always strapped," but even when they are broke they always find ways to "pay the prosecutor."

"We've failed tragically to realize Gideon's promise because of the unwillingness of state and local governments to adequately fund the defense function. . ." said Steven Benjamin, former president of the NACDL, the National Association of Criminal Defense Lawyers. "The system is broken. It can't be relied upon to protect innocent people from conviction."

In another article on the anniversary of the *Gideon* decision, Karen Houppert of Morgan State University cited Mark Twain's joke about the American legal system: "The law is a system that protects everyone who can afford a lawyer."

That was true in the nineteenth century, and it is sadly still true in the twenty-first century, as Dewayne's case proved. The lack of adequate counsel, combined with prosecutorial misconduct, produced a miscarriage of justice that almost killed an innocent man.

As we have seen, there is good reason to believe such injustices occur in about 4 percent of capital punishment cases. Yet according to Justice Scalia, there's nothing unconstitutional about it. According to Scalia, it would have been constitutional for the state of Texas to kill Alfred Dewayne Brown, despite the fact that he had nothing to do with a heinous crime that somebody else committed. That's just the way things were in Scalia's America. Not in mine.

And increasingly not in others' as well, including those from the right. Former Texas Governor Rick Perry, who signed over 300 death warrants during his fifteen-year tenure, including the warrant for Cameron Todd Willingham, recently spoke at the annual meeting of the American Legislative Exchange Council (ALEC), and gave a speech entitled: "Black Lives Matter – and So Does Black Liberty." He specifically referenced Dewayne's case as an example of prosecutorial misconduct and a broken criminal justice system. He said:

> You could say this story has a happy ending, because Alfred was released. But his life was almost ruined because of an overzealous prosecutor who concealed exonerating evidence. And Ericka's children were put in harm's way because of a grand jury that acted as the arm of the prosecution, rather than as an independent check on government power. . . . Anyone wielding the power of the state faces the temptation to abuse it. And when it comes to prosecutors, there are clearly bad apples in the system who care more about indicting someone—anyone—than they care about convicting the right person.
>
> You may know that I was indicted in 2014 on two frivolous felony charges. Eventually, those charges were dismissed, because I was lucky enough to have high-powered lawyers working for me.
>
> Ericka Jean Dockery had no such luxury. When ambitious prosecutors go overboard, the true victims aren't people like you or me: they're people like Ericka and Alfred who don't have the means to fight back.

I couldn't have said it better myself. Thank you, Governor Perry, for standing up for Dewayne.

Chapter 13:

The Defense Bar

"Dewayne maintains his innocence. He refuses to sign for a crime he did not commit."

District Attorney Rizzo decided to try Elijah Joubert and Dewayne separately, with Joubert on trial for Alfredia Jones's murder and Dewayne on trial for Officer Clark's murder.

Joubert was tried first in October 2004. Glaspie testified against his accomplice. In court, Rizzo played a videotape of Ghetto's confession. Joubert's defense was that, while he was present during the robbery, he did not have a gun with him, so he should only be found guilty of aggravated robbery. The jury deliberated for an hour and rejected that defense. They found him guilty, and recommended a death sentence.

With Joubert's conviction and sentence secured, the media coverage was extensive for Dewayne's trial. It was going to be difficult to find jurors who had not heard about the case and who could be fair and impartial. The court brought in and examined three large pools of people, 395 in all. Of those 395, twelve were selected as trial jurors, with two alternates.

In his opening statements, given on October 10, 2005, Rizzo declared the case was a "tragedy" in which a twenty-year veteran of the police force who was on the verge of retirement and a young mother who was coming back to work after maternity leave were killed. He asserted that Shon, Ghetto, and Dewayne tried to rob one check-cashing store and were thwarted, so they settled on robbing the ACE location. He told the jury about the evidence he planned to present, including Shon's testimony, telephone calls between the men on the date of the incident, and testimony that would be given from eyewitness accounts, including Ericka Dockery and Sharonda Simon, Dewayne's current and former girlfriends, respectively. He asked the jurors to "wait and see" the evidence. "We believe that you'll be able to find this defendant guilty beyond a reasonable doubt," he concluded.

Loretta Johnson Muldrow stood up to deliver the opening statement for Dewayne.

As a criminal defense attorney, I have seen many different types of lawyers in my work, some good ones and a lot of bad ones. Slick operators in pinstripe suits and too much gel in their hair who represent mobsters, drug dealers, and other seedy characters for gobs of cash. "Ham and eggers" in mismatched suits from J. C. Penney who hang around the courthouse and pick up low-level misdemeanors and handle DWI cases for five hundred bucks a case. Young, spirited public defenders who truly believe in the mission, work long hours, and fight tenaciously for their clients, but usually burn out and go to private firms or quit the law altogether. Grizzled old public defenders, who don't care all that much about what they are doing and are beaten down by the system. To be sure, I have seen many good defense attorneys and worked with a number of them, but overall, I think I have seen more bad and beaten-down ones than good ones.

Loretta Muldrow did not obviously fit into any of these categories. She was not a public defender. Unlike many other jurisdictions, Harris County did not have a formal public defender system at that time for capital murder trials, meaning that the County did not have employees who were paid to represent poor people charged with crimes. All of the indigent defendants were represented by private attorneys willing to take the appointments from the Court for a set hourly fee, which varied by the type of crime. In 2015, the rate for defending a client in a capital case is $150 per hour. It was far less than that in 2005, when Dewayne was tried. This in itself demonstrated the inequality built into the American justice system. In New York, you got a public defender if you jumped a turnstile in the subway. In Houston, if you allegedly killed someone, you had to rely on the good graces of a court-appointed private attorney who agreed to take your case on a reduced fee.

I want to be fair to Muldrow. She had colleagues who spoke highly of her, and she likely provided competent counsel in other cases. She was up against a prosecutor willing to engage in tactics of which she had no knowledge. And she was not well compensated for her work. But those facts cannot excuse the defense in Dewayne's case.

Before the trial, Muldrow did not move for a change of venue outside of Houston where jurors would not be influenced by the pervasive news coverage the case received in Houston. She received but did not adequately investigate evidence that Dewayne was not the third man at the crime scene. She did not investigate his alibi by securing evidence of his whereabouts. In court, she made inconsistent arguments, did not effectively cross-examine witnesses, and failed to fully challenge unreliable hearsay presented in court as factual evidence. She did not put on any evidence at all during the defense case; she rested without calling a single defense witness. She also failed to disclose that she had long been a law partner with Dashan Glaspie's attorney, a serious conflict of interest.

In her opening arguments, Muldrow focused on the theme of "mere presence," meaning that her argument was that Dewayne was at the scene of the crime, but did not participate in the offense. He was, according to Muldrow, "merely present," but not guilty of anything. She argued that Shon and Ericka Dockery had every motivation to "follow the script" given to them by Rizzo about the case, but that case, she told the jurors "will be wholly, wholly insufficient for one reason and one reason only: Alfred Dewayne Brown is innocent."

The "mere presence" defense was extremely troubling. It contradicted Dewayne's repeated statements that he was not at the crime scene. Dewayne did not agree that this should be the defense strategy and said over and over again he was not there. Both Muldrow and her partner in the defense, Robert Morrow, knew Dewayne's repeated position that he was sleeping at Ericka Dockery's apartment when the crime took place, not that he was "merely present" at the scene.

They heard his position many times when they urged Dewayne to take the plea bargain. In a note written on July 16, 2004, Morrow wrote that "D continues to insist he wasn't there, there [sic] case is not overwhelming but, with Shon flip [agreement to plead guilty and testify against Dewayne], certainly strong enough." Morrow noted that he wanted to "review with Loretta." Another note stated: "Dewayne maintains his innocence, and *He refuses to sign for a crime he did not commit.*" (Italics in original notes).

There was no question as to Dewayne's position regarding the crime, but Muldrow and Morrow persisted with the "mere presence" defense anyway. Dewayne had legal counsel as guaranteed by *Gideon* but he did not receive the legal counsel contemplated by *Gideon*. As a result, he did not receive justice.

Chapter 14:

Defense Fail

What follows are summaries of the testimonies of virtually all of the witnesses in the case, in the order they testified. I will focus on the more important witnesses such as Ericka Dockery, Dashan Glaspie, and Sharonda Simon, and try to be even-handed about what was said for both sides, so readers can make their own determination about the state's case. At the same time, I will add vital information that did not surface at the trial.

As I say in every opening statement to the jury, "Ladies and gentlemen, please keep an open mind and don't make your decision until you have heard all the facts in this case." That is all I ever ask of jurors, and that is all I can ask of you.

The first witness was Talana Townsend, a service associate for ACE Cash Express. She talked about the procedure for opening up an ACE Cash Express location and the robbery code used by Ms. Jones, "opening store 24." She was the one who called the police, and the 911 call was played for the jury.

Roland Baylous, a twenty-nine year veteran of the Houston Police Department and personal friend of Officer Clark, testified that the robbery call was a "Code 1" call requiring immediate response. Baylous was miles away, so Officer Clark responded. Baylous heard Clark say, "He's got a gun, step it up," on the radio call. The next radio call he heard was, "Officer down."

D. C. Lambright, a crime scene investigator for the Houston Police Department, took the stand to describe an aerial photograph of the incident scene. He testified that there were shell casings from .380- and .45-caliber weapons recovered from the scene. Lambright said Clark's handgun had jammed at the scene of the incident. When questioned about the process of lifting fingerprints from a crime scene, Lambright said that a "very low percentage" of fingerprints can actually be used. "What you see on TV is not exactly true," he reminded the jurors, concluding the first day of trial.

The second day began with the testimony of Kevin Carr, a Homicide Division investigator with the Houston Police Department. He authenticated the bullet that was recovered from Officer Clark's body.

Kenneth Walden took the oath. He was an insurance salesman whose office was located near the first check-cashing store on Telegraph Avenue that was approached that morning. He said he saw a white Pontiac Grand Am back into a parking spot in the strip mall, occupied by three black males, two in the front of the Grand Am and one in the rear. He did not identify Dewayne as one of the men.

Leo Foisner told the court that he arrived at his check-cashing store at about 7:30 a.m. the morning of April 3, 2003. He was speaking to a customer on a bicycle as he was about to open the store, when he saw two young black males come across the parking lot toward him. He said that he took out his pistol, cocked it, and flashed it at the approaching men. The men immediately changed direction, he said. Foisner did not identify Dewayne as one of the men.

Another eyewitness was James Wheat, the truck driver who heard a call about the ACE robbery over his police scanner. He followed Officer Clark, whom he had known for years, to the strip mall. He heard Clark say, "Step it up. They have guns." In the parking lot, he noticed a white Grand Am, and also saw a red Grand Am. He did not hear any gunshots. He saw three black males run out of the ACE, get in the white Grand Am, and drive away. He was not close enough to make an identification of the men. He did not get the license plate number of the car. He ran to the store after the men left, found Officer Clark and Ms. Jones, and called for help on Clark's radio.

Stepping to the witness chair next was Lisa Hubbard. She was key to Rizzo's case. Hubbard testified that at about 8:00 a.m. on April 3, 2003, she saw Dewayne at the VA. He was with Shon and Ghetto in the parking lot near a car. Shon and Ghetto were on one side of the car talking, and Dewayne was on the other side of the car. She said that it was unusual for them to be up that early in the morning. When she walked by Shon and Ghetto, she said she heard Ghetto ask Shon, "Are you ready to go do this?" Hubbard testified that when she heard this, she "knew they was about to go do something they didn't have any business doing."

Hubbard said she then went into the apartment of her friend Tonya Barnes, and they cooked breakfast and watched television. About thirty minutes later, when she came out of Barnes's apartment, Shon was standing by the driver door of the car, loading bullets into the clips for his gun. He put one clip in the gun and the second clip in a briefcase. Hubbard testified that she later talked with George Powell ("Ju-Ju"), who told her that "they really went and did it."

That's when she started thinking about the reward money. She called in a tip to the Houston Police Department about Shon, Ghetto, and a man named "Deuce." She said she mentioned Deuce because he was also at the VA that morning. When she went to a lineup, she saw Dewayne and suddenly remembered that he had been at the VA that morning as well. Hubbard testified that she received a $10,000 reward from Crime Stoppers for her work on the case.

To her credit, Muldrow raised the issue of her changing story on cross-examination. Hubbard admitted that her first statement to the police did not include any references to Dewayne. She said her first witness statement was incorrect. She said that she didn't read what the police gave her to sign, she "chose not to" sign it because she was "tired . . . I was ready to go home." She acknowledged that she received the Crime Stoppers money only after she went to the lineup and changed her story to implicate Dewayne by stating that he was with Shon and Ghetto on the morning of the incident.

Lisa's sister, LaTonya, took the witness oath. She said that she and her friend Letisha Price walked her daughter to school between 7:00 and 8:00 a.m. Hubbard said she and Price then stopped at a gas station on Alameda and Telephone Road. They saw Shon and Ghetto standing by the white Grand Am. She said Price talked with Ghetto. She said there was a third man present who "had on all black, a black hooded jacket with, I think, a little red or white or something on the sleeve of it." She said she could not see the man's face because of the hood. She told the police she thought the third man was Deuce. She said that she had seen Dewayne in the lineup later that day but did not recognize him as someone she saw earlier that day. She said that she no longer thought the third man was Deuce because she was unable to see his face, but she didn't say it was Dewayne. She testified that she also received a $10,000 Crime Stoppers award.

The next witness was George Powell, or "Ju-Ju," and he was, shall we say, less than convincing. Powell readily testified that he drank "morning, noon, night," and mixed Xanax with alcohol "all the time," and he blacked out sometimes. He said he stayed up all night the night before the incident, then went to the store to get some cigarettes at about 6:30 or 7:00 a.m. on the morning of the incident. Rizzo asked if he was already stoned on that morning when he went to the store. Powell said yes, he was "getting there."

"What you were getting there on at the time?" Rizzo asked.

"I was on the bike going to the store," Ju-Ju said, and the courtroom erupted in laughter.

When he returned to the VA, Ju-Ju said that he saw Shon, Ghetto, and two other men standing near the white Grand Am. Dewayne was not there, he said.

"I didn't—I didn't see Doby none that morning."

Powell remembered that when the car came back after the incident, Shon and Ghetto got out of it, and he could not be sure if anyone else got out, because he "already was kind of tipsy." He testified that he never saw Dewayne get out of the car. He said Shon gave him the .45-caliber gun to hide.

Rizzo dismissed Powell's story, pointing out that he had made contradictory statements to the police regarding Dewayne's presence at the VA on the day of the incident. Rizzo played a tape of him answering questions where he gave a different statement.

"It didn't happen like that, though, but on the tape recorder, yes, it's on the tape recorder," he stammered. "But it didn't happen like that." The policeman was "trying to make me say what he wanted me to say."

Powell, Rizzo told the judge, was "clearly feigning memory loss."

On cross-examination, Powell again testified that he did not see Dewayne with Shon and Ghetto earlier that morning. Near the end of Powell's examination, he said, "Say your Honor, can I plead the Fifth—man?" Obviously frustrated, Judge Ellis adjourned the court for the day.

Chapter 15:

Prosecutorial Misconduct

The lethal combination of inadequate defense and prosecutorial misconduct converged in the courtroom on the third day of trial.

It started with Sharonda Simon, Dewayne's former girlfriend and mother of his daughter, Kiearra. She was Dewayne's only child. Simon told the court that she saw Shon, Ghetto, and Dewayne at the VA at about 10:30 a.m. on the morning of the incident, standing near Shon's Grand Am. Shon was near the driver's side, Ghetto in front of the car, and Dewayne sitting in the rear, she said.

On cross-examination she admitted that there were lots of people standing by the Grand Am, and she never saw Dewayne get out of the car. But Muldrow did not ask her where she was when she observed the men and the car. In fact, Simon was standing a hundred yards away when she saw the crowd around the car, a distance that made conclusive identification difficult, if not impossible. I know this because I stood exactly where she said she saw him. The defense had missed an opportunity to expose the weakness of the state's case.

The court then heard from three witnesses who live in the VA regarding how Shon's gun was recovered. They said Ju-Ju Powell had sold the gun to a VA regular for fifty dollars. The gun was then put in a trash bag for a while, and then in a diaper bag in a closet, where it was recovered. None of the witnesses about the gun saw Dewayne on the day of the incident.

Darrell Robertson, a police officer with the Homicide Division of the Houston Police Department, testified about the physical evidence that was found at the scene. On cross-examination, Officer Robertson confirmed that the initial tips that came in on this case involved "Ju-Ju, Ghetto, Little Red, and Deuce." He also confirmed that during one lineup Dewayne was in, LaTonya Hubbard was unable to identify him. Finally, he confirmed that Deuce was never put into a lineup because he had an alibi—he was with his girlfriend—which was not the most original or convincing of explanations.

Police Officer Lorenzo Verbitskey recounted Shon's arrest at the motel for the jury. He said that he took a gunshot residue test on Shon's hands on the afternoon of April 4, 2005. The test has a two-hour window of effectiveness and more than twenty-four hours had passed since the crime, he said, so the test was negative.

Walter Stairhime, Jr., from the Identification Division of the Houston Police Department, explained that he had processed the crime scene looking for latent fingerprints and found none matching with the fingerprints of Ghetto, Shon, and Dewayne.

The trial was about to reach a turning point. Alma Berry, the elderly woman who employed Ericka Dockery, came forward to testify. She said that Ericka typically came to her house at 9:00 a.m., and stayed either four or five hours. She said that she had met Dewayne twice before, and recognized his voice when he called to talk with Ericka. Around 10:15 a.m. on the morning of the incident, she recalled that she answered the phone and it was Dewayne, calling to talk with Ericka. She said Ericka had told her to turn on the news, which was reporting the shooting. She saw on TV a few nights later that Dewayne had been arrested, and she fired Dockery.

On cross-examination, Berry was asked about whether she recalled telling Dockery, "It's your house," when the phone rang. She denied that she said that.

It was a decisive moment—and it passed unnoticed, because Rizzo said nothing. In fact, he knew of evidence that the call did in fact come from Ericka's house. The evidence was Southwestern Bell's record of calls made from Dockery's landline phone number that day. The record—which would not surface until 2013, when it was found in a Houston Police detective's home garage—showed that at 10:08 a.m. on April 3, 2003, a call was made to Alma Berry's house from Ericka Dockery's house.

Rizzo himself signed a subpoena requesting the records from the telephone company on April 24, 2003. That was the day after Ericka testified in the grand jury about the call. It seemed that Rizzo was trying to figure out if she was lying or telling the truth when she testified about the call—and he obtained evidence that she was telling the truth. Nonetheless, he charged her with perjury, sent her to jail for four months, and chose not to turn over the phone record to Muldrow and Morrow, as required by *Brady*. Rizzo did investigate Dewayne's alibi, in fact he confirmed it, and he allowed testimony to the contrary to be admitted against Dewayne.

The district attorney's conduct did not merely originate in his misguided personal mission for winning a conviction over doing justice. Rizzo was enabled by a judicial system that virtually never sanctions prosecutors for *Brady* violations or other forms of misconduct. In his 2013 dissent about the "epidemic of *Brady* violations," Judge Alex Kozinski wrote that "a robust and rigorously enforced Brady rule is imperative because all the incentives prosecutors confront encourage them not to discover or disclose exculpatory evidence. Due to the nature of a Brady violation, it's highly unlikely wrongdoing will ever come to light in the first place. This creates a serious moral hazard for those prosecutors who are more interested in winning a conviction than serving justice."

"In the rare event that the suppressed evidence does surface," Kozinski went on, "the consequence usually leaves the prosecution no worse off than had it complied with *Brady* from the outset. Professional discipline is rare and violations seldom give rise to liability for money damages. Criminal liability for causing an innocent man to lose decades of his life behind bars is practically unheard of."

In Dewayne's case, the exculpatory evidence did not surface for nine years— all of which Dewayne spent behind bars—and the district attorney would face no consequences for his actions.

So, too, with prosecutors who have sent—and continue to send—men and women to death row in recent decades. In a recent case that was profiled on *60 Minutes* on October 11, 2015, a prosecutor in Louisiana, Marty Stroud, confessed that he sent an innocent man, Glenn Ford, to death row for nearly thirty years. Ford was the longest-serving death row inmate in America. Stroud said that he was "arrogant, narcissistic, and caught up in the culture of winning," in which key evidence was suppressed and he ignored other suspects in the crime. When another confessed to the crime, Ford was released. He was released in March 2014 and died of lung cancer on June 29, 2015. He died penniless, relying on local charities to take care of him, because the state denied him compensation for the time he was on death row. Stroud has asked the Louisiana State Bar to discipline him. I was encouraged and heartened by Stroud's coming forward, but that won't give Ford his thirty years back.

Whether by pure misguided zeal or actual misconduct, prosecutors have immense power and face limited consequences if they exercise that power in an unfair or illegal way, no matter what *Brady* requires. As Kozinski noted, "When a public official behaves with such casual disregard for his constitutional obligations and the rights of the accused, it erodes the public's trust in our justice system and chips away at the foundational premises of the rule of law. When such transgressions are acknowledged yet forgiven by the courts we endorse and invite their repetition."

The exposure of prosecutorial immunity is indeed eroding the public trust in the justice system in general, and in the capital punishment system in particular. It is another reason why the death penalty is dying in America.

Chapter 16:

Ericka's Story

The fourth day of trial was dominated by Ericka Dockery and her testimony—shaped by pressures from the district attorney and uninformed by the withheld phone record. The story she told was immensely damaging to Dewayne. Dockery told the jury she was thirty years old and recently married. She had three daughters: Tyecia, who was thirteen; Patrice, who was ten; and Carlissia, who was eight. She had completed eleventh grade in high school and earned a GED. She said she was going to school to get a job in medical insurance billing and coding.

She said she had lived with Dewayne for six months prior to the incident. She said that she took drugs routinely, including cough syrup laced with drugs, marijuana, and ecstasy. She testified that she was charged with aggravated perjury because she "lied to the grand jury." She said that she was high when she spoke to the grand jury and lied to protect Dewayne. She recounted living in jail for four months on the perjury charges because she could not make bail. She said she accepted a plea deal because she "wanted to go home. I wanted to tell him everything that was going on and to go home."

On the night before the incident, she said she and Dewayne had a fight because he said he was going to see his friend at the VA that evening. She told him not to come back and went to bed. She said she did not sleep well because of the argument, and woke up late. When she went downstairs, Dewayne was asleep on the sofa in the living room. She tapped him on his shoulder and asked him what he was still doing there. He looked at her, smiled, and went back to sleeping. Ericka said her young cousin Ruben Jones was playing video games in the big chair in the living room next to where Dewayne slept.

Ericka drove the kids to school. When she returned home at 7:25 a.m., Dewayne was gone, she said. She then went to work at Ms. Berry's house. She said she next heard from Dewayne around ten o'clock when he called Ms. Berry's house. She said that Dewayne told her he was calling from "the VA at Shondo's house or something like that," and that they resumed their bickering from the night before.

Dewayne then told her to change the TV to the news.

"Put it on Channel 26," he said. "Something happened over there by your house."

The TV correspondents were talking about the killings at ACE Cash Express.

Ericka said she saw Dewayne again when she returned from work in the afternoon, but he said he was sick and didn't feel good. She said that his behavior was unusual and he looked nervous. They took a nap together, and she got up in time for her shift at Subway that evening.

Ericka testified that she got a series of phone calls the next day from Dewayne's sister, his brother, and Sharonda Simon about Dewayne. She said she knew that Dewayne had gone to the police station to talk about the incident. After Dewayne was arrested, she visited him in jail almost every day, and repeatedly asked him whether he was involved in the crime. He always denied it. During those jail visits, however, Dockery said that Dewayne apparently told her to lie to the grand jury, and say that he was home at 8:30 a.m. on the day of the incident. She said that she then started getting calls at her house.

Dockery then testified that the final time she went to visit Dewayne in jail, she asked him again whether he was involved. This time, she said, "he looked at me, put his head down and looked at me." She said that he said, "I was there. I was there."

Because of this statement, she said that she never spoke with him again.

During cross-examination, Muldrow asked about Dockery's jail time. She said that there were more than thirty women in the jail, some sleeping on the floor. The toilets were out in the open and she rarely got to see her daughters. She said it was an absolutely terrible time.

Muldrow asked her about her drug use. She said she took drugs almost every day, including "syrup," or liquid codeine, and lovacel, a muscle relaxer, as well as ecstasy, marijuana, and Xanax. "It ain't nothing to pop a pill," she testified. "Just put it in your mouth, drink some water and keep on stepping."

Muldrow asked about the phone call she received at Ms. Berry's house. Muldrow did not know about the phone records of Ericka's landline because Rizzo had withheld them. But she had made little, if any, effort to locate them herself, so she didn't have them to cross-examine Ericka or present to the jury. In any case, she did not have any more questions, and Ericka Dockery was excused.

Chapter 17:

The Accomplice's Story

"Without speaking to someone personally, there's no way you can know who spoke to who on a certain call, absolutely."

It was Dashan Glaspie's time to testify. But before he took the stand, Judge Ellis told the jury that Shon had been charged as an accomplice, or someone who participated in the crime. A conviction, he explained to the jurors, could not be based on accomplice testimony alone. The accomplice's testimony had to be "corroborated by other evidence tending to connect the Defendant with the offense committed." This protection makes sense and protects a defendant from getting convicted on "snitch" testimony alone.

Shon's self-serving account, which saved him from the possibility of the death penalty, was devastating to Dewayne. Not only did he say that Dewayne was the third man at the crime scene, he all but said Dewayne had shot Officer Clark.

Shon testified that on Tuesday, April 2, 2003, he told Ghetto that he was looking at a check-cashing store on Telephone Road and that he wanted Ghetto to come along with him and see what he thought about it. Shon then spoke with Dewayne at the VA that evening. Shon testified that he asked Dewayne to come along to watch outside the door.

"Me and Ghetto was going to go in and I just wanted him [Dewayne] to look out, basically," and make sure no one came inside. He said Dewayne agreed to be a part of it.

The next morning Shon was at a motel room with Tonikia Hutchins, his girlfriend at the time, who drove a white Grand Am. At approximately 6:00 a.m., Shon left the motel with Hutchins. They went to her father's house. At approximately 6:40 a.m., Shon called Ghetto, who was at the VA. He told Ghetto he was on his way. Then he called Dewayne at Ericka Dockery's house. A "younger dude" answered the phone, he said.

After Shon dropped off his girlfriend, he drove to Ericka Dockery's house and picked up Dewayne. They went to the VA, where Ghetto got into the backseat of the car. They went to the Crystal Springs apartment complex so that Dewayne could get a jacket from his brother A.B.'s house. Shon, Ghetto, and Dewayne then drove to a gas station near the check-cashing store on Telephone Road. He said Dewayne and Ghetto walked towards the store where an older white male was talking to another older white male on a bicycle while he stayed in the car. His two friends turned around and returned to the car. Ghetto said that the white male "let his gun be seen," so they decided not to rob that store. They went back to the VA to regroup.

At the VA, Shon said that Dewayne used Shon's cell phone to call his brother A.B. and Sharonda Simon. Dewayne then walked to Simon's house, he said. After about twenty minutes, Shon went to pick up Dewayne. It was time to go rob the ACE store.

When they arrived at the ACE Cash Express store, Ghetto asked whether Shon had his .45-caliber automatic with him. Shon said he did, and it was under the seat in the car. Ghetto grabbed it. Shon and Dewayne went into a furniture store, while Ghetto stayed in the car. Shon said Ghetto had said that when the store employee drove up to open the store, he was going to use the gun to walk her inside.

Shon testified that he and Dewayne stayed in the furniture store for "around fifteen, eighteen minutes, somewhere." They talked to an older man who Shon thought was "Iranian," about furniture and prices. While Shon talked to the store clerk, Dewayne walked around in the store. Dewayne then walked out of the store and Shon followed.

When he and Dewayne walked out of the furniture store, Shon said Ghetto was no longer in the Grand Am. Shon said he put on a hat and jacket and walked to the check-cashing store. He said he went in through the front door of the store and then through the first mantrap door, or a series of locked doors that customers had to pass through to get to the inside of the store. (These are the kind of setups you see at high-end jewelry stores, or low-end pawnshops or check-cashing places, where you are locked into a small area with a locked door behind you and a locked door in front of you until someone buzzes you in).

Shon said that Dewayne was already in the store at the second mantrap door, and he held the door open for him. He said Ghetto was in the back of the store by the safe pointing the .45 at the store clerk, Alfredia Jones, who was kneeling. Ghetto told her to open the safe. She said she did not know the code. The store phone rang. Shon told Ghetto not to let Jones answer it. Jones said that she needed to answer it to open the store. Ghetto told her to answer the call, while pointing the gun at her. Shon remembered that Jones mostly just said "yes" and "no" to the caller. Shon said he was looking around for security cameras, while Dewayne was looking through Jones's purse.

A minute or so later, they heard a police radio and saw a police officer walking towards the front of the store. Shon ducked down. He said Ghetto had Shon's gun, but he did not see whether Dewayne had a gun. Dewayne went towards the front door, Shon said, and he heard shots. The only possible implication was that Dewayne shot Officer Clark even though Shon never said he saw Dewayne actually do the crime

At this point, Jones said, "Why y'all doing this? Why y'all robbing this place?" Ghetto said, "P, this bitch played us," and shot her. Ghetto then went out to the lobby and Shon went out behind him.

On the way out, they saw the police officer lying in the doorway. Shon said that when he got into the Grand Am, Dewayne was already in the driver's seat. Ghetto got in and Dewayne drove off. Shon said that a chrome automatic was sitting on the back floorboard, along with Shon's .45.

They went back to the VA, he said, and parked near Nikki Colar's apartment. Ghetto grabbed the .45 and Dewayne grabbed the other gun. They went inside, changed clothes, and threw their other clothes into a dumpster. Shon let Dewayne use his cell phone, and then Dewayne left. Shon called his girlfriend to pick him up. He said he did a dope run, delivering the drugs to a regular customer on the southwest side. Then he and his girlfriend checked into a motel. That's where he was when he was arrested.

On cross-examination by Muldrow, Shon was questioned about who was at Dockery's house when he went to pick up Dewayne. He said it was an "older woman," and assumed it was Dockery's mother (there was no older woman at Ericka's house). When asked about his police interrogation, he acknowledged lying to the police multiple times. He admitted that he recently bailed Ghetto out of jail on a $2,000 bond. He said he robbed the ACE Cash Express store because he needed some money to replenish what he had just spent on the bond.

Muldrow questioned Shon on his plea deal. He acknowledged that he met with the prosecutor between five and ten times to go over his testimony.

"So you knew what you had to do, right?"

Shon said no.

On redirect examination by the state (the state gets to ask questions of their witnesses after the defense cross-examines the witness, most often as an attempt to rehabilitate the witness or clear up statements from the cross-examination),

Shon acknowledged that he lied to the police for a "few hours." He also said he was close to Ghetto and that he thought that Ghetto did what he did at the crime scene by accident rather than intentionally.

On recross examination by Muldrow (not always allowed, but sometimes the defense gets another shot at the witness after the state conducts its redirect if they raise a new issue), Shon confirmed that he did not see Dewayne with a gun inside the store. She then referred to Shon's testimony as a "script." She asked no further questions.

Another key witness came when Officer Breck McDaniel took the stand. What he did and didn't say bolstered the state's case against Dewayne.

What McDaniel *didn't* say was that he knew about the phone call from Ericka Dockery's landline to Ms. Berry's house. The phone records that Rizzo did not share with Dewayne's lawyers were found in 2013 in Officer McDaniel's home garage. A home McDaniel shared with his wife, a District Attorney who worked with Rizzo. The words "Doby GF landline" were handwritten on the record, most likely by McDaniel. "Doby" referred to Dewayne and "GF" (girlfriend) referred to Ericka. McDaniel said nothing about this phone call in his extensive and detailed testimony, which focused almost exclusively on phone records. The word irony doesn't do justice to the situation. A better one would be offensive. Or illegal.

Officer McDaniel illustrated his testimony with a series of maps of Houston that showed where and when certain cell phone calls were made. Muldrow and Morrow knew about the maps and objected before McDaniel took the stand. Made by a technique called "cell phone triangulation" (remember this is 2005, when cell phone GPS technology was in its infancy), the maps displayed the location of the cell phone towers through which the calls were made, along with photographs of the person that police believed had made the calls. Literally, there was a picture of Dewayne next to a series of calls to show the jury that he had made the calls. The defense objected because, aside from Shon's testimony, there was no way to truly know who made or received the calls.

"That objection is overruled," Judge Ellis said, without explanation.

These maps should not have been admitted into evidence. The only "evidence" of a call between Dewayne and someone else was Shon's testimony, which was speculation based on a review of the phone records and where the call went. The cell phone maps were the only way the district attorney could link a small slice of "scientific" evidence to Dewayne. If Shon said, "Dewayne called so and so" or "that call must have been Dewayne calling someone," then that supposition was illustrated on a map that was blown up for the jury. With Dewayne's face next to the location of the call, it looked official. It looked like he made the call. In a case that was very short on forensic evidence, the cell phone maps were critical. They were, in essence, large posters that allowed the state to speculate about who made the calls. The jury was led to believe they constituted evidence, when in fact they were hearsay.

Officer McDaniel started with an account of the lineup where Dewayne and the other defendants were brought before various witnesses. He said that Mohammed Afzal, the furniture store employee, made a "tentative" identification of Dewayne.

He then presented the maps that showed the times of various calls made on the day of the murders, the approximate locations, and the photos of the person who made and received the calls.

Officer McDaniel stated that between 8:45 a.m. and 10:14 a.m., there were no calls between the men. After 10:14 a.m., McDaniel testified about other calls, including a 10:17 a.m. call from Shon to his friend Jessie Coleman and some calls between Shon and Ghetto.

On cross-examination, Officer McDaniel was asked about the lineup of suspects. He said that some of the witnesses did not identify Dewayne as a participant, including Letisha Price, James Wheat, and LaTonya Hubbard. Lisa Hubbard only recognized Dewayne from the VA, but not from the day of the murders.

Regarding the phone records, Muldrow said the cell phone records "won't show who actually placed the call and who actually answered the phone." Officer McDaniel responded "absolutely," and "without speaking to someone personally, there's no way you can know who spoke to who on a certain call, absolutely."

Muldrow cross-examined Officer McDaniel with one hand tied behind her back. She didn't have the phone record. And Officer McDaniel did not offer a tour of his garage. She had no additional questions.

The murder of Alfredia Jones was the most despicable and tragic part of the ACE Cash Express murders. Officer Clark was a threat to the perpetrators. He was armed and fired a shot at them. Alfredia Jones was not armed and posed a threat to no one. And she was killed anyway.

Jackie Vital, a district supervisor for ACE Cash Express who supervised the store that was robbed, testified that Jones had worked for ACE for four years. She was a "floater" who worked in any store in Vital's district. Vital confirmed that Jones had just returned from maternity leave when she was killed.

As for the crime, Vital testified that the alarm company had provided records of the exact times that the front door of the store and mantrap doors inside were opened. The records showed that three people entered the store and that Officer

Clark arrived at the scene less than three minutes after Ms. Jones's alarm, and likely died within a minute of his arrival. They showed that the second person to enter the store was there for less than four minutes, and that the third person to come in was there for less than two minutes.

The last witness was Sheikh Mohammed Afzal, the sixty-eight-year-old furniture store employee, who said that "two black guys" came into the store on the morning of the murders and looked at bedroom furniture. In identifying Dewayne, he said, "based on my memory I saw him in the furniture store that day." When he was asked whether he was 100 percent sure, he said, "No, I'm pretty sure, sir." When he was asked to quantify how sure he was, he said, "Well, I will be about 80, 85 percent."

Afzal said that he talked to one of the men, and he was "pretty sure" it was Dewayne. He said Dewayne asked him about the price for some bedroom furniture. The two men were in the store for two to three minutes, he said, and then left. He went to a police lineup, and said that he recognized Dewayne but was only about 85 percent sure of his identification.

Under cross-examination by Muldrow, Afzal stated that he met with the district attorney three to four times regarding his testimony. Muldrow played a tape recording of Afzal's statement to the police in which he said that he did not see the way the men left the store because he "was busy with paperwork." Afzal then acknowledged that when he went to the lineup, he said, "I'm not 100 percent sure. It might be number three" (where Dewayne was standing). Muldrow then insinuated that Rizzo suggested to Afzal whom to select.

On redirect examination, Rizzo played the entirety of what Afzal said in the lineup, which included the statement that "[h]e came in for a few minutes and looks to me number three."

"Did I ever get you to try and identify anybody?" Rizzo asked. Afzal said no.

On recross examination, Muldrow summarized Afzal's testimony: "So you went from not 100 percent sure, might be, to I think it seems to be, to a maybe, to an 85 percent sure today; isn't that correct, sir?" He said yes.

After Afzal was done, the state rested its case. That was the evidence against Dewayne. All of it. No forensics, no scientific evidence of any kind. Some alleged witnesses, an ex-girlfriend, a snitch, and some bogus posters.

It was then time for the defense to present its case. Time to tell their side of the story. Time to fight back. Muldrow stood up and said, "We would have no evidence to offer." The defense rested without putting on a single witness. No alibi witness, no fact witnesses, nobody. Nothing. The jurors were sent home for the weekend.

Chapter 18:

Closing Arguments

"Good luck with that, this is Texas."
*"If I had done just a smidgen of what Ms. Muldrow said, I should not
only be fired, but I should be indicted."*

During my practice as a criminal defense attorney I have often seen all the participants in the system—the prosecutors, the defense attorneys, and the judges—
lose sight of the important constitutional functions they all play and become
players in a ritual that repeats itself over and over.

The prosecutor wears the white hat as the self-righteous protector of the victims and infallible arbiter of justice who demands a certain result. The judge typically bows to the prosecutor's desires, and the defense attorney shouts from the
rooftop, begging for mercy, or just sits there and takes it. Everyone sleeps well at
night because most, if not all, of the participants believe that the guy is guilty of
the offense, and even if he isn't guilty of *that* crime, the prosecutor likely believes
that he is guilty of *something*, especially if he is from a minority group, poor, and
has a prior record. All of this is fueled by an overall perception of who the "bad
guys" are who should be put away to protect society.

When you spend enough time in a courtroom, you can see and feel this current of "justice." It is a stream that sucks in and carries along all the participants,
like fish swimming along with the current.

I saw the stream firsthand when I went to a court hearing early on in Dewayne's
case. The courtroom was filled with downtrodden defendants and their lawyers,
and a smug, cocky prosecutor presided over the courtroom like he owned it.
When I was waiting for Dewayne's case to be called, I saw him look at Dewayne's
file and say, "Man, when the hell are they going to get an execution date on that
damn case? Dude needs to go." I stared at him, gave him a very mean Jersey
look, and said, "There will **NEVER** be an execution date in that case, my friend."

He got his back up, stared right back at me, made a "pfff" sound, flicked his hand at me, and said, "Good luck with that, this is Texas." After the court hearing, I walked right by him and said, "I'll be back," like I was Arnold frickin' Schwarzenegger. I didn't flow in the stream that day.

But the stream worked the way it usually did in Dewayne's trial, flowing to its inevitable conclusion.

The initial closing argument for the state (they go first and get a rebuttal after the defense gives its closing) was done by Tommy LaFon, Rizzo's trial partner.

"You'll understand it becomes clear that this was a horrible, horrible crime where two honorable people are no longer walking the face of this earth because of what these guys did," he told the jurors. "Today is judgment day and it is the responsibility day for this Defendant."

LaFon then described the "law of parties," which means that when three people commit an offense, they act together, and each has a role and responsibility in the case; they are all guilty of the offense. He then addressed the "mere presence" defense by saying that, "It's not just that this Defendant was present with these guys. It's that there is more evidence than that. There is participation." He said that Dewayne was in the check-cashing store, went through Alfredia Jones's purse, and ultimately shot Officer Clark. This was far from being "merely present" at a scene, he said.

Dewayne's conduct, he said, was "sick," it was "weird," it was "very unusual," and "it's certainly not consistent with the evidence of an innocent man who was just merely present." Dewayne's statement to Ericka Dockery, "I was there," did not indicate mere presence, he argued. It showed he was guilty.

Robert Morrow began the closing arguments in Dewayne's defense. He said that the jury had to make a decision about whether Dewayne shot Officer Clark. He then said that, "If you don't feel he was the shooter, there's no evidence to prove him guilty as a party or as a conspirator," therefore the "only verdict you can come to is not guilty."

Morrow then turned the argument over to Muldrow.

"I'm going to dive right in, and I've spent the last twenty-four hours writing it down so if I seem a little bit off the path, it's because I haven't had a whole lot of sleep," she began. "But, trust me, I'm going to get my point across by the time I sit down."

She said that Shon could not be believed in the case because he told "well over one hundred lies." As for Ericka Dockery and the Hubbard sisters, she said, "You ask yourself if the witnesses have any particular reason not to tell the truth. Twenty-two months on curfew, 120 days in that cesspool called the Harris County Jail. Ten thousand dollars for women who were not working, [and] two capital murder charges dismissed."

Muldrow noted the lack of scientific evidence against Dewayne: no "forensic items, no prints, no DNA, no ballistics, no weapon ever seen on Mr. Brown. No forensic evidence to tie Mr. Brown. Mr. Brown does not own a cell phone and Ericka Dockery did not have one, either." The cell phone records, she noted, didn't show who actually placed or received the calls.

The witnesses had been told what to say by the prosecutor, she argued. "The problem is you dress these witnesses and rehearse them for this man's trial. When you do that, they're no longer witnesses. They're tools."

Muldrow challenged Dockery's testimony, stating that "anyone who has ever had a child—you don't have to bear them. If you've just ever held a little cub in your arms, you'd know you'd rather go to hell and back before you separate yourself from your cub. You know this, right? You wouldn't do it. Ericka Dockery had 120 days' worth of reasons to shade her testimony for Dan Rizzo."

Muldrow closed by saying, "Alfred Dewayne Brown does not have any sufficient proof of guilt for one reason and one reason only. It's not just insufficient. Okay. It's in their own forensic evidence. He's innocent. He's innocent because he was at home."

So over the course of the four-day trial, Dewayne's two lawyers had changed the theme of his defense from "mere presence" at the crime scene to "he was at home." Which was the jury to believe? Dewayne's attorneys offered no help. They did not call a single defense witness or present any evidence.

Rizzo delivered the state's rebuttal argument, which was less about what Dewayne did or did not do on April 3, 2003, than about Muldrow's personal attacks against him. They were sleazy, he said. "I'm not going to go on and comment about those other than to say that they are offensive. They're terribly offensive to me as a prosecutor for this long a period."

"Ladies and gentlemen, " he went on, "if I had done just a smidgen of what Ms. Muldrow said, I should not only be fired, but I should be indicted. So what she did to you was, she lied." The irony continues—if the jury knew that Rizzo had stashed away the exculpatory phone record, his indictment could have been a real possibility.

To accuse a defense attorney of lying is a very improper statement to make in a closing argument. I have never seen or heard—and likely never will—such statements in a closing argument. Muldrow objected and Judge Ellis overruled her.

When Rizzo finally calmed down and addressed the evidence, he said Officer Clark was a hero (one of the only things Rizzo said that I agree with). "We're here, ladies and gentlemen, because of him. We're here because of what he did . . . all of us lost a little bit, a little bit of our security, too, knowing that people like this actually exist."

"What kind of person could do that?" He paused, turned, and pointed to Dewayne.

Rizzo said that Shon had the most to lose, and therefore had the most incentive to testify truthfully. He explained the lack of forensic evidence by saying, "What it does is it shows you that TV is not exactly—the things on CSI and all those shows is not exactly the way it works."

He described Muldrow's "mere presence" defense as nonsensical.

"You can't say, 'You know, I just happened to be in the back near the cashier while these two good friends of mine had picked me up and that I just happened to be there and I was only present. . . . It doesn't make any sense." He was right, it didn't make any sense.

"Ladies and gentlemen, police officers are human," Rizzo concluded. "And we know that they feel. We know that they get mad. They get sad. We know that they get scared. And we also know that they bleed and they die. They put their lives on the line every single day for us because they're the only thing that stands between us as a community and people like this. . . . When the evidence supports, ladies and gentlemen, that we have the cop killer here in the Court, we must, under the law, find him guilty."

Chapter 19:

The Verdict

The jury was excused to begin deliberations. Over the next few hours, the jury asked the judge for clarification on two points.

First, they wanted to know what time Dockery testified that she got to Alma Berry's house on the morning of the incident. The judge read the portion of the transcript that stated that Dockery got there between 8:30 and 9:00 a.m. This showed how important Ericka's testimony and timing was to the jury.

Second, the jury sought clarification as to whether Sharonda Simon testified that she talked to Dewayne on the phone on the day of the incident. The judge stated that there was no testimony regarding any telephone conversation between Simon and Dewayne.

The jury was paying close attention to the evidence. Could Ericka Dockery have left her house at 7:20 a.m., taking over an hour to get to Alma Berry's house? Or was she not telling the truth about when she left? Was Shon lying when he said that Dewayne talked to Sharonda Simon using his cell phone, a claim that just so happened to fit the state's presentation of the phone records and the colorful maps?

It all didn't seem to matter at the end of the day. The next day, the jury returned to the courtroom with a verdict:

"We, the Jury, find the Defendant, Alfred Dewayne Brown, guilty of capital murder as charged in the Indictment."

Chapter 20:

Ratifying Injustice

"He is a gentle giant with a humble spirit."

The jury was instructed to come back the next morning to decide whether Dewayne should be put to death.

In Texas, as in most states, the jury that decides guilt or innocence also decides the punishment. In capital cases, the jury can decide to impose the death penalty if there are "aggravating factors" in the case, such as when someone presents a threat of future danger to the public. The jury can also decide that there are "mitigating circumstances" that compel the jury to give a life sentence. Before Texas permitted life without parole sentences in September 2005 (it was the last of the death penalty states to do so, and Harris County prosecutors opposed it to the end), a life sentence meant that a defendant would be eligible for parole in forty years. That choice put jurors in a very difficult position, as there were fears about potentially letting violent individuals back into society, albeit many years later. This dilemma contributed to the high number of death sentences in Texas for many years, and I am sure it is why Harris County prosecutors did not want the life-without-parole option, as it almost guaranteed a "win" in every capital case. Predictably, however, once life without parole became a sentencing option, juries gave that punishment far more than they gave death sentences. In fact, a December 2015 *Dallas Observer* article was entitled "Texas Falls Out of Love with the Death Penalty, Embraces Life Without Parole." While death sentences plummeted to single digits annually, life-without-parole sentences rose to near one hundred each year.

In the punishment phase, the jury also hears victim impact statements about the effects of the crime on the family and friends of the victim.

In Dewayne's case, as in other death penalty cases, both the "expert" testimony and the victim impact statements did not serve the cause of justice.

Rather, they served to ratify the miscarriage of the justice that took place during the criminal trial.

The state went first and called witnesses to address Dewayne's other alleged criminal conduct to argue that Dewayne was a danger in the past and the future and should receive the death penalty.

Ibrahim Ali-Saab was the first to take the witness stand. Ali-Saab was a witness because Dewayne allegedly robbed him prior to the ACE robbery. The state wanted his testimony to show that Dewayne was a violent person and committed other robberies. Ali-Saab initially testified outside of the presence of the jury because Morrow objected to his testimony and sought to question him before he was able to testify in front of the jury.

Ali-Saab testified that he was the victim of a robbery at the OST Food Market, a convenience store in Houston, on March 31, 2003, four days before the incident at ACE Cash Express. He said that there were three suspects, one of whom came behind the counter during the incident. He looked at Dewayne and said, "Maybe it's him," and then said, "It's him." He testified that the police asked him to review the videotape of a lineup that Dewayne was in. The first time he reviewed the tape, he did not identify anyone. The second time he reviewed the tape, he identified Dewayne.

On cross-examination, Morrow asked whether the identification was based on the fact that Ali-Saab's coworker at the store saw Dewayne's picture in the newspaper in connection with the ACE robbery, and that made him believe that Dewayne was one of the individuals who robbed him. Ali-Saab acknowledged that he was not 100 percent sure of his identification. Morrow restated his objection, arguing that the testimony was not strong enough to be put before the jury on such a critical issue of prior alleged violent acts. Nevertheless, the judge allowed the identification to come into evidence. Ali-Saab would be called as a witness later in the punishment phase.

Officer William Cowles, Jr., who investigated the OST Food Market robbery, said that an OST employee, Michael Jabbour, saw pictures of the suspects in the ACE murders and believed they were the men who robbed him. Officer Cowles met with Jabbour, and showed him a photo array, which included Dewayne, Shon, and Ghetto. Jabbour identified Ghetto and Shon, but not Dewayne. Cowles also showed Jabbour the videotape lineups that included Dewayne. He identified Shon and Ghetto, but again, not Dewayne. Cowles then spoke with Ali-Saab, who identified Dewayne.

Michael Jabbour took the stand. He said he was working at the back register of the OST when one of the men grabbed him and said, "You SOB, come back and give me all the money." Jabbour then said that he was struck in the head with a "good size" pistol. As he lay on the ground, one of the men put his foot on Jabbour's back. Jabbour had over $7,000 in cash in his pocket, because he was going to make a down payment on a home. He gave it to one of the men and later identified that person as Shon. Jabbour stated that he was able to identify Shon and Ghetto from the photo arrays and the videotape lineups. He did not identify Dewayne as one of the robbers.

Officer James Rachel of the HPD testified about how Dewayne came to be implicated in the holdup. He said that when he showed Ali-Saab the video lineup that included Dewayne, Ali-Saab initially did not make a positive identification. Ali-Saab did make a positive identification of Ghetto and a tentative identification of Shon, he said. Rachel said he showed the video lineup including Dewayne again to Ali-Saab, admitting that it was not common practice to show the lineup twice. After that second viewing, Ali-Saab made a positive identification of Dewayne.

Ali-Saab returned to the witness stand. He was now permitted to testify to the jury. Ali-Saab testified that he saw Dewayne come behind the counter at the robbery at the Food Market.

"Yeah, I see him, but he change, I mean." Dewayne was different, he said, because he was "a little heavier today than he was that day."

That was important because by that time Dewayne had been in custody for months, and had lost weight pending his trial. If anything, he would have been heavier when he was allegedly in the OST Food Market, and not the other way around. The videotape of the robbery was played for the jury. Ali-Saab testified that he viewed the videotape of the lineups and said that he didn't identify anyone the first time. On second viewing, he said he was 85 percent sure he could identify Dewayne. By the way, I saw the video, and the gunman was not Dewayne at the robbery. There was no resemblance. It was not even close.

Even though the testimony was not strong at all, just the allegation that Dewayne was involved in another robbery likely had a reassuring effect on the jury. If they had any doubts about their guilty verdict, they probably felt much better hearing from a witness who said Dewayne had committed another robbery right before the murders.

Prosecution witnesses also sought to depict Dewayne as a drug user. Officer Richard Morales of the Houston Police Department recounted a previous incident involving Dewayne. He said that on January 8, 2002, he stopped a car for two reasons. The car had no front license plate, and the passenger in the front seat was not wearing a seat belt. When Morales approached the car for the traffic stop, he said he saw the driver throw something out of the window. He found a small brown vial with PCP and smelled the odor of marijuana. Dewayne was the driver of the car. When Morales searched Dewayne, he found six pills in his pocket. They were later determined to be amoxicillin, an antibiotic.

The passenger in the car, Dashan Glaspie, was searched, and marijuana cigarettes were found on him. Shon had an open warrant for escape from a juvenile detention facility. Both Dewayne and Shon were taken into custody. The dope was Shon's, but Dewayne did the time. He served seven months in jail for the PCP possession charge.

Then the families of the victims had their time. Kenneth Jones, the forty-one-year-old brother of Alfredia Jones, testified that his sister was the youngest of six children in the family. He said she had two children, a ten-year-old boy and a newborn girl, who were now being raised by their grandmother. The boy was now in counseling about his mother's death, he said. He described his sister as very outgoing and said she was missed very much at family gatherings. She was "smart," "kind," and "affectionate." She was his "buddy," his "pal," and he was overly protective of her. Alfredia had taken maternity leave, and was just starting back to work again when she was killed.

Marlene Keele, younger sister of Officer Charles Clark, said she worked for the Harris County Sherriff's Department. Her big brother, she said, was one day shy of his twentieth anniversary at the Houston Police Department on the day he was killed. He was "quiet, shy," "very caring," and a "very steady-type person." When she found out from her husband that her brother was dead, she said she "just collapsed." She said she was suffering from depression and had a recurring nightmare in which she was riding with her brother to respond to the robbery call. When he got out of the car in the dream, she yelled at him to come back. Then she saw him being shot.

In another dream, she went on, she saw "my family members and my best friend, me being in uniform, watching them get shot," and "they've all been shot by the same person." She pointed to Dewayne.

Morrow objected, saying that her testimony went outside the scope of the notice that prosecutors had given to the defense about what the witness would say. The state is obligated to give notice to the defense about the victim impact testimony. Nowhere in the notice did prosecutors disclose that Officer Clark's sister would say she had a recurring dream in which Dewayne killed other family members.

"I think every juror in the box was weeping, asking for Kleenex—with an allegation that Mr. Brown had killed all these people in her dreams," he said, asking for a new sentencing hearing with a different jury. Judge Ellis denied the motion.

It was time for the defense sentencing presentation. In his opening statement to the jury, Morrow raised the issue of intellectual disability (some state laws, including Texas's at the time of the sentencing in Dewayne's case, used the term "mental retardation," but for the purposes of this book I will use the preferred term of "intellectual disability" unless directly citing from an expert report or the judge for accuracy purposes), saying Dewayne's IQ was in the "sixty-nine to low seventies range."

"Dewayne has never really been able to do more than write his name," he contended. "Dewayne can't read because of severe learning disabilities which have shaped his life and which are beyond his control." He said the evidence would "show that this young man, with his limited functioning, his learning disabilities . . . is not a candidate for . . . death row."

His first witness was Cat Brown, Dewayne's mother, who testified that Dewayne was a "quiet baby." He was one of four children. She identified some pictures from when Dewayne was little. She testified that Dewayne was sent to live in Louisiana, where he helped his uncle on a crawfish pond and hauling wood. He lived with his maternal grandparents: loving, caring people who raised eleven children in a modest home and did it the hard way, sharecropping for very little money and living off the land.

Dewayne was later brought back to Houston so he could be with his mother and siblings. When he was growing up, she said Dewayne did not have a lot of friends. "He was always by himself." He didn't speak until he was about five or six. They called him "Sugarbear" because he looked like the bear on the Super Golden Crisp cereal box.

Donald Randall, Dewayne's uncle, said that he and Dewayne had "good days working together." He identified pictures of Dewayne working on a crawfish boat, and other locations in Louisiana. He said Dewayne struggled in school and was very bad with money. After one workday, he recalled that he paid his son with four five-dollar bills and Dewayne with a twenty-dollar bill. He said Dewayne thought that he had given his son more money. He gave Dewayne his nickname, "Dough-B," because he was heavy as a child.

Two of Dewayne's former teachers testified. Marcus Broussard, a teacher in the Saint Landry Parish in Louisiana, said that when Dewayne was fourteen years old, he was reading "somewhere around a first grade reading level." He noticed that Dewayne was easily taken advantage of.

Elnora Malveaux, a teacher's aide, testified that Dewayne "was a very friendly person, always had a smile on his face." He couldn't read much, she said, "just the little simple words like 'the,' 'was,' 'this,' and 'that.'" He liked to spend time with the children in the kindergarten class, where they would write letters on the blackboard together.

The jurors also heard from Dewayne's grandmother and an aunt and uncle, who told more stories about Dewayne's childhood. They called him a "gentle giant" with a "humble spirit."

The defense then called its experts to try to convince the jury that Dewayne was intellectually disabled and therefore could not be executed. The Supreme Court ruled that someone with an intellectual disability could not be given the death penalty, so this aspect of the case was critical.

The first witness was Dr. Jim Patton, a professor at the University of Texas in the Department of Special Education. He said that Dewayne's Louisiana school records indicated he was "qualified under the category of mild mentally disabled." Dr. Patton explained that "mild" means the "highest functioning of individuals with mental retardation." To diagnose intellectual disability, he explained that he relied on three major-pronged analysis: (1) a sub-average IQ test; (2) deficits in adaptive behavior, or how well one deals with the demands of everyday living; and (3) evidence that the condition occurred prior to age eighteen.

Dewayne's school records, he said, showed that at age eleven, his IQ score was seventy-one. His score on the Vineland test (an adaptive behavior test which analyzes a person's communication skills, daily living skills, and socialization) was sixty-nine, Dr. Patton said, which was two "standard deviations below the mean." That meant that a "very small percent of people will have that score and below," he explained. Dr. Patton said that he had interviewed fourteen people about Dewayne, including family members, friends, and former teachers, but was unable to make a formal diagnosis that Dewayne was intellectually disabled.

"There's information in the records that indicate that certainly mild mental retardation is a possibility here," he said. "And there's enough evidence, I think, to certainly pursue that. My interviews did not provide me with the supportive information that I like to have."

The next witness was Dr. Dale Watson, a psychologist with training in neuro-psychology and intellectual assessment. He said Dewayne's school records indicated a 95 percent probability that Dewayne's IQ was between sixty-seven and seventy-eight. IQ scores of seventy-five or below will be considered to be within the intellectually disabled range or at least consistent with a diagnosis of retardation, he said. Dewayne was "very poor at dealing with most verbal information," he explained. "That's his real weakness. He just doesn't deal with language very effectively."

Dr. Watson's conclusion was that Dewayne had brain damage.

"We know his IQ is very bad," he said. "He was slower than virtually everybody. You know, he's in the bottom 2 percent of the population. He cannot read or write because of brain damage or maybe some developmental dysfunction of some sort. He forgets both verbal and visual information rapidly. He cannot use language effectively for communication. He can—don't get me wrong, I don't want you to misunderstand. He can communicate very simple things, but complex thinking is really beyond him. He's slow at even simple tasks. So that even things that most people would be able to do really rapidly, he's slow at. And then he shows signs of left hemisphere brain dysfunction."

Dr. Watson said that he lacked sufficient information on adaptive deficits, so he, like Dr. Patton, could not make a formal diagnosis of intellectual disability.

On cross-examination, Rizzo also asked Dr. Watson whether Dewayne had "the ability to plan to go and commit a robbery." Dr. Watson stated, "I think the basics of a robbery, he probably could plan. I don't think it would be a very sophisticated plan," adding that "people with mental retardation can—they can commit crimes."

The first witness called by the state in rebuttal was Dr. Patton, the defense witness. Rizzo asked Dr. Patton to review the notes from his interview with Dewayne. In those notes, it reflects that when Dr. Patton spoke with Dewayne about what he did in his free time, he responded that he watched television, played dominos, and played chess. Rizzo asked whether chess was a more sophisticated game than checkers. Dr. Patton said yes.

The state then called Dr. George Denkowski, an expert who has testified for prosecutors in many death penalty cases. As subsequent events would show, he was a fraud whose testimony should have never been admitted.

Chapter 21:

In the Tradition of Dr. Death

"He scored 68 but that was not a valid indication of his actual mental ability because of moderate to severe depression and . . . mild anxiety. He could not perform optimally on the test."

The use and abuse of expert witnesses in America's capital punishment system has a long and sordid history. While these pseudo-experts have condemned many to die, their actions have also served to discredit death penalty jurisprudence and undermine its future existence.

One so-called expert who testified in several Texas death penalty cases was Dr. Walter Quijano. In 1997, he was asked about the "future danger" posed by Duane Buck, a black man convicted of killing his ex-girlfriend and a friend of hers. On cross-examination, the prosecutor said to Dr. Quijano, "You have determined that the sex factor, that a male is more violent than a female because that's just the way it is, and that the race factor, black, increases the future dangerousness for various complicated reasons. Is that correct?"

"Yes," Dr. Quijano said. The state's "expert" said the man would be a danger in the future because he was black. Duane Buck remains on death row in Texas in the Polunsky Unit, where Dewayne was.

In 2000, then-Texas Attorney General (now U.S. Senator) John Cornyn identified seven cases, including Buck's, in which the state of Texas impermissibly relied on Dr. Quijano's testimony linking the race of defendants to future dangerousness. Cornyn acknowledged that reliance on testimony connecting race to dangerousness was wholly unacceptable and promised that the Attorney General's Office would seek new, fair sentencing hearings for these seven men. Nevertheless, Buck remains on death row, but in June 2016, the Supreme Court agreed to hear his case, and it will be decided in the term starting in October 2016.

Even more notorious was Dr. James Grigson, who died in 2004. Nicknamed "Dr. Death" for his willingness to testify against capital murder defendants, Grigson was a witness in hundreds of death penalty cases. As the *Houston Chronicle* reported after his death, "his pleasant manner, down-to-earth vocabulary, and air of certainty helped persuade juries that the defendant—just about every defendant—would kill again if given the chance. That Grigson often had not met with the defendant did not deter him from forming an opinion about him and defending it to the hilt."

Grigson's willingness to make absolute judgments earned him the praise of prosecutors and the scorn of professional psychiatric organizations, the *Chronicle* said. He was twice reprimanded by the American Psychiatric Association, which eventually expelled him as a member. So did the Texas Society of Psychiatric Physicians.

In the case of Randall Dale Adams, convicted of the 1976 murder of a Dallas police officer, Grigson labeled Adams an "extreme sociopath," despite Adams's lack of a criminal record. Grigson said there was no doubt he would kill again, even in prison. Adams, whose case was featured in the documentary film, *A Thin Blue Line*, was later exonerated after another man confessed. Adams did not commit any offenses after his release, and he lived a quiet life, married to the sister of a death row inmate, until he died of a brain tumor in 2010.

In the tradition of Doctors Grigson and Quijano, Dr. Denkowski could be relied on to say what death penalty prosecutors wanted to hear. He testified that he was a clinical psychologist specializing in evaluation and diagnosis. He said he began working with intellectually disabled individuals in 1954 and had served as chief psychologist for the Fort Worth State School for intellectually disabled students. He testified that he worked on approximately sixteen cases involving a capital murder defendant who was facing the death penalty, and testified in seven or eight of those cases. Of the sixteen cases he worked on, he said that he found that six defendants were intellectually disabled, and ten were not.

The issue of intellectual disability and the death penalty has a very sad and unfortunate history in this country. In 2002, the Supreme Court banned executing those with intellectual disabilities in what has become known as the *Atkins* decision (the case name is *Atkins v. Virginia*). Prior to *Atkins*, states (except for Maryland and Georgia, because they banned the practice) were able to execute defendants with intellectual disabilities. And states did exactly that. According to the Death Penalty Information Center, forty-four defendants with intellectual disabilities were executed from 1976-2002. Even after *Atkins*, there were instances in which defendants were executed who were suspected to have intellectual disabilities. Consider the case of Warren Hill in Georgia. Although Georgia was obligated to follow *Atkins*, it set a high bar—beyond a reasonable doubt—for Hill to prove his intellectual disability claim. Every doctor who examined Hill determined that he had an intellectual disability. A judge found that Hill did have intellectual disability, but not to the "beyond a reasonable doubt" standard required by Georgia law. The family of Hill's victim opposed his execution, citing his intellectual disability. Former jurors from the case advocated for life without parole. Former President Carter advocated for a commutation of life without parole.

None of it mattered. Hill was executed on January 27, 2015 and pronounced dead at 7:55 p.m. Hill's lawyers called the case a "grotesque miscarriage of justice" and "rendered the Eighth Amendment a mere paper tiger."

Sadly, Hill's case is not alone—just two days after Hill was executed, Texas executed Robert Ladd, who had an IQ of sixty-seven. According to his attorney, Ladd's intellectual disability was "well documented, debilitating, and significant." That was a despicable and embarrassing week for our country.

Dr. Denkowski sought to continue this unfortunate legacy. For Dewayne's case, Dr. Denkowski said he asked Dewayne approximately three hundred to four hundred questions to determine how Dewayne functioned. He also administered an IQ test, and tests for reading and writing abilities. Then he spent approximately five hours making a diagnosis and writing a report. He concluded that Dewayne did not meet any of the three criteria for intellectual disability: low IQ, adaptive deficits, and onset before age eighteen.

Regarding Dewayne's life skills, Dr. Denkowski stated that Dewayne did not live in a "very organized home setting" until he moved to Louisiana, where his grandmother and uncle helped him and taught him things. He did not score well on basic life skills and socialization at age eleven because he had not yet had the guidance and support of his Louisiana family. When a child is "from an underprivileged or neglected background, they're just not going to know these things and they're going to come out low on this—on these adaptive behavior skills," he said. "But it doesn't mean that they do not have the ability to learn, to learn the skill or the ability to know when to perform the skill. It's just a learning deficit."

Dewayne scored very high on his communication portion of the skills test, Dr. Denkowski said, which was unusual because intellectually disabled individuals typically perform poorly on that aspect of the test.

Dr. Denkowski said he gave Dewayne the Wechsler Adult Intelligence Scale IQ test, the most widely used test to determine adult intellectual functioning. The benchmark for intellectual disability was generally accepted to be seventy, and most states set that number as the line for being eligible for executions. The Supreme Court invalidated that rigid line in 2014, so a person with a seventy-one would not automatically be eligible for execution. But it was 2005 when Dewayne was sentenced, so seventy was the magic number. He scored sixty-eight, but that was "not a valid indication of his actual mental ability because of moderate to severe depression and . . . mild anxiety." Dewayne, he said, could not "perform optimally on the test."

Because of his depression and anxiety, Dr. Denkowski said he adjusted Dewayne's IQ up to a range of seventy-two to seventy-seven, getting him above the seventy threshold for intellectual disability. He did this purportedly because of "clinical judgment based on my experience with depressed people and IQ testing." He then stated that he had used this procedure in prior cases.

On cross-examination, Morrow asked whether there was any evidence that Dewayne was "malingering," or faking, during the testing. Dr. Denkowski said there was no evidence of faking. Morrow challenged Dr. Denkowski's use of the depression scale to elevate Dewayne's IQ score, stating that studies have questioned that approach. Dr. Denkowski acknowledged that he had made errors in his testing on occasion, and the reduction from sixty-nine to sixty-eight was an error that was caught by the defense experts.

After Dr. Denkowski completed his testimony, Morrow called Dr. Watson back to the witness stand to address Dr. Denkowski's testimony. Dr. Watson stated that there is no support in the medical literature for raising Dewayne's IQ score because of alleged depression. Dr. Denkowski was relying on "outdated research," Dr. Watson said, and stated that more recent studies, including one from 2003 (the hearing was in October 2005), that show that "depression has been shown to have no impact on IQ scores."

After hearing from one more witness, a woman who lived in the VA who said she did not think Dewayne was intellectually disabled, the evidentiary portion of the punishment hearing was over. It was time for closing arguments on whether Dewayne was going to die.

Chapter 22:

The Four Issues

"He's trying to let these people take my life away for something I didn't do."

Judge Ellis explained to the jurors that they had to address four issues in deciding whether to sentence Dewayne to death:

(1) Whether Dewayne would commit criminal acts of violence that would constitute a continuing threat to society;

(2) Whether Dewayne intended to cause the death of Officer Clark, or, if he wasn't a shooter, did he anticipate a human life would be taken;

(3) Whether Dewayne suffered from "mental retardation;" and

(4) Any other special mitigation issues regarding his case.

After these instructions, the lawyers gave their final arguments to the jury. Morrow argued first for Dewayne.

"We want to see a fair punishment based on the facts," he said, insisting "we're not asking for mercy," and "we're not asking for forgiveness." Life in prison was the proper punishment, he said, because Dewayne's low IQ "affects his ability to function." He argued that Dr. Denkowski didn't like the results of Dewayne's IQ test, so he had tried "to explain that away" with the depression issue. Morrow also questioned the strength of the OST robbery evidence, stating that it was not sufficiently proven that Dewayne had anything to do with the crime. He agreed that the families of Officer Charles Clark and Alfredia Jones had been severely hurt by their deaths.

Morrow then addressed the special issues. First, Morrow said that Dewayne had not committed any acts of violence while in custody, and there was no evidence showing that he would be a danger to society. Second, Morrow said that there was sufficient doubt about Dewayne's role in the case, particularly because of Shon and Ghetto's roles in the other robbery, which called into question Shon's truthfulness about his role in this case. Regarding intellectual disability, Morrow said that Dewayne was "mildly mentally disabled," citing the "honest testimony" of Dr. Patton and Dr. Watson.

Muldrow concluded the defense's argument by urging the jurors to "give fair and impartial consideration to the full range of punishment." If sentenced to life in prison, Dewayne would not be eligible for parole for forty years. "Death is final," she said. "You don't get a second chance at your decision. So, it must be the right one."

Rizzo gave the first part of the state's closing. He said that he did not want the jurors to vote "because of emotion." Even though Dewayne had a difficult childhood, Rizzo said he was lucky that he had family in Louisiana who cared for him.

"Of course" Dewayne was a future danger, he said. He intended to take Officer Clark's life because he shot him at close range in the head. Regarding intellectual disability, Rizzo stated that none of the experts had stated that Dewayne was intellectually disabled, so the dispute between the doctors about how the tests were done was irrelevant. It was "ridiculous to think this person is retarded," he said, noting that Dewayne played chess. Rizzo closed by saying Dewayne was a "violent predator," a "person who preys on people . . . who doesn't care about other people."

LaFon continued the prosecution's closing. The evidence supported the death penalty, he said. He urged the jury not to be swayed by the innocent pictures of Dewayne's youth, but to focus on Dewayne's actions as an adult.

All of a sudden, in the middle of LaFon's closing, according to news reports, Dewayne "raised his hand like as if he was a student in class, stood up and said in a pleading, shaky voice":

> "Excuse me. I didn't rob nobody. I didn't shoot nobody. . . . These people trying to take my life away for something I didn't do. I'm tired of sitting up in here . . ."

Muldrow hugged Dewayne and pulled him back to his chair. The jury was excused.

Dewayne continued:

> "These people trying to take my life away for something I didn't do. I didn't do this crime, man. It's hard sitting up in here.

He's trying to let these people take my life away for something I didn't do."

Rizzo asked that Dewayne be removed from the courtroom before another outburst, and the guard took him away to a holding cell. Muldrow and Morrow left to speak with him. When Dewayne was brought back into the courtroom, Judge Ellis said, "Mr. Brown, you cannot say anything for the balance of the argument. It's not allowed."

"Yes, sir," Dewayne responded.

"I understand you have feelings and want to express them," the judge went on. "I understand that. But you simply cannot, under the rules, do that. If you say anything else, I'll put you in the holdover [the holding cell behind the courtroom] for the balance of the argument."

"Yes, sir," Dewayne said.

LaFon resumed his closing argument. The OST robbery, he said, showed that the same team who did the ACE Cash Express robbery was responsible for that robbery. They got a "taste for that quick, easy money that day," so they set out to rob the ACE.

As for the question of intellectual disability, LaFon stated there was "no question" that Dewayne could not read or write "as a result of a learning disability." But the defense had "muddied the waters" with experts who could not provide an intellectual disability diagnosis. LaFon defended Dr. Denkowksi, stating that he has had a career dealing with intellectually disabled people and evaluating them, and he does not always find that the person he is evaluating is not intellectually disabled. His rationale could be trusted in this case.

"You understand that this is a person with a learning disability, an inability to read and write, and that is bad, it's tragic. . . . But the truth is he's not mentally retarded," he said. "There's nothing about a learning disability that affected his choices in that matter."

"The truth is there are people like this Defendant out there who are waiting on people to make one mistake," he summed up. "It's the time you leave your door unlocked or your window unlocked. . . . There are people out there waiting for you to make the one mistake so that they can exploit it and take advantage of it."

The "result of this Defendant's actions is that there is two kids that don't have a mother anymore, one child who was an infant when her mother died. . . . A wife that doesn't have her husband. A family that doesn't have their brother. The law enforcement community that lost a comrade. HPD, who lost a valued, experienced employee one day before his twentieth anniversary. All because of this Defendant and his buddies."

"When you kill a police officer, there should be a consequence," he said. "I'll trust that you'll make the right decision."

The jury retired for the evening. The next day, on October 25, 2005, the jury returned a verdict. The verdict sheet stated:

> Special Issue No. 1: Do you find from the evidence beyond a reasonable doubt that there's a probability that the Defendant, Alfred Dewayne Brown, would commit criminal acts of violence that would constitute a continuing threat to society?
>
> Answer of the jury: We the jury, unanimously find and determine beyond a reasonable doubt that the answer to this special issue is yes.
>
> Special Issue No. 2: Do you find from the evidence beyond a reasonable doubt that Alfred Dewayne Brown, the Defendant himself, actually caused the death of C. Clark on the occasion in question or if he did not actually cause the death of C. Clark, that he intended to kill C. Clark or that he anticipated a human life would be taken?
>
> Answer of the jury: We, the jury, unanimously find and determine beyond a reasonable doubt that the answer to this special issue is yes.
>
> Special Issue No. 3: Do you find by a preponderance of the evidence (a lesser standard than beyond a reasonable doubt) that the Defendant, Alfred Dewayne Brown, is a person with "mental retardation"?
>
> Answer of the jury: We, the jury, unanimously find that the answer to this special issue is no.
>
> Special Issue No. 4: Do you find from the evidence, taking into consideration all of the evidence, including the circumstances of the offense, the Defendant's character and background, and the personal moral culpability of the Defendant, Alfred Dewayne Brown, that there is a sufficient mitigating circumstance to warrant that a life sentence rather than a death sentence be imposed?
>
> Answer of the jury: We, the jury, unanimously find that the answer to this special issue is no.

The jury was polled, meaning that each of them had to audibly say "yes" when they were asked whether this was their verdict. Once that was done, the verdict was entered.

The judge then spoke to Dewayne:

"Mr. Brown, the jury having found you guilty of the offense of capital murder, and by the answers to their questions having assessed your punishment at death, it is my order that you be delivered by the Sheriff of Harris County to the Director of the Institutional Division of the Texas Department of Criminal Justice, where you will be confined until the date of your execution. It will be set by this Court after an affirmance by the Texas Court of Criminal Appeals, if that should come to pass."

Dewayne was escorted out of the courtroom.

The families of the victims expressed relief. "The relationship between the Jones and Clark families will last forever," said one of the relatives as they left the courthouse.

Dewayne was taken to Harris County Jail. His next stop was death row.

Day of Dewayne's arrest. He went to the police station to clear his name in April 2003 and was arrested and charged with capital murder.

The scene of the crime: ACE Cash Express, Houston, Texas

The victims of this senseless and terrible crime. Officer Charles Clark was a decorated twenty-year veteran of the Houston Police Department and Alfredia Jones had just returned from maternity leave to work at the ACE Cash Express. I often pray for their families.

Elijah Joubert was convicted of the murder of Ms. Jones and is currently on death row. Dashan Glaspie pled guilty to aggravated robbery and received a thirty-year sentence.

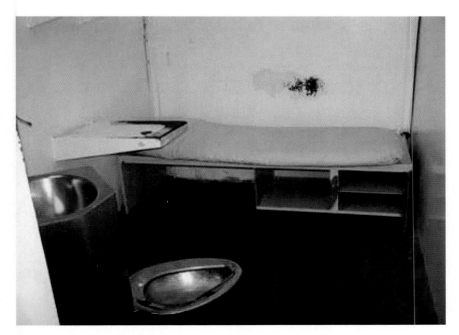

An example of a death row cell at the Polunsky Unit—Dewayne was in his cell for twenty-three hours a day during the week and twenty-four hours a day on the weekend. His one hour out of the cell was in an enclosed rec yard. Dewayne said it was like going from the "dog kennel to the bird cage."

One of many legal visits to death row—the best part was being able to buy Dewayne vending machine food and to talk with him about his life. Our brotherhood started here.

Affidavit of Elijah Dewayne Joubert

1. My name is Elijah Dewayne Joubert. I reside at the Polunsky Unit in Livingstone, Texas. I was convicted of capital murder on October 21, 2004 for the events at ACE check cashing on April 3, 2003.

2. I have personal knowledge of the facts and circumstances before, during, and after the incident at ACE check cashing on April 3, 2003.

3. Alfred Dewayne Brown was not involved in any way with the incident on April 3, 2003 nor present at the ACE check cashing store on April 3, 2003.

4. In fact, I did not see Alfred Dewayne Brown on April 3, 2003.

5. I swear under the penalty of perjury that the foregoing is true.

Dated: 4-22-08   _Elijah Joubert_
                        Elijah Dewayne Joubert

Notary: _Ruby Singleton_
        4-22-08

Ruby Singleton
Notary Public, State of Texas

Affidavit from Elijah Joubert stating that Dewayne was not involved in the crime.

APPLICATION

COMES NOW, the State of Texas, by and through her Assistant District Attorney, Dan Rizzo, and hereby request that an Order be signed requiring the herein named utility to furnish all Verbatim Call Records, including all incoming and outgoing call activity for the listed telephone number. And, to furnish to the Homicide Division of the Houston Police Department, through the below named officer, as soon as practical and at reasonable intervals during regular business hours, for the duration of this Order.

I.
The utility is Southwestern Bell Telephone Company (SBC)

II.
The subscriber is Monea Pickett. The telephone number is 713-649-6385

III.
The location of the instrument is 6969 South Loop East, Houston, TX 77087

IV.
The release of said telephone records are material to the investigation of a criminal offense; supporting information follows:

The subpoena requested by DA Dan Rizzo the day after Ericka Dockery testified in the grand jury about the call to her workplace coming from Dewayne at her house, and the phone record that confirmed it. The phone record was not provided to Dewayne's defense attorneys at trial. It was uncovered in May 2013 in the home garage of a Houston Police Department officer who worked on Dewayne's case. It was the evidence that proved Dewayne's alibi and set him free.

B8 | Wednesday, June 10, 2015 | Houston Chronicle | HoustonChronicle.com and chron.com

HOUSTON ★ CHRONICLE

FOUNDED 1901 · A HEARST NEWSPAPER

PAUL BARBETTA, *Executive VP and*
JACK SWEENEY, *Chairman*

An innocent man

Justice is upheld by the DA dropping charges against Alfred Dewayne Brown.

The Texas Code of Criminal Procedure states that it is the primary duty of all prosecuting attorneys "not to convict, but to see that justice is done." With her announcement Monday that charges would be dropped against Alfred Dewayne Brown, Harris County District Attorney Devon Anderson has done her duty.

disagrees.

Houston Police Chief Charles McClelland has reiterated in public statements that he still believes Brown is guilty, as has Officer Joseph Gamaldi, the police union's 2nd vice president. The police union Twitter feed also continues to refer to Brown as a "murderer."

Officers like McClelland and Gamaldi

Houston Chronicle editorial after Dewayne's release. *Chronicle* reporter Lisa Falkenberg won the paper's first Pulitzer Prize for her work on Dewayne's case.

Release day. Dewayne finally got to hug his daughter, Kiearra, who was two years old when he was arrested. Also pictured are Dewayne's sister Connie, and death penalty abolitionist Pat Hartwell.

Dewayne addressing the media after his release. Dewayne said that he "went there as an innocent man and I came out as an innocent man." He also said that he does not have hatred in his heart for the years that were taken away from him. With him is Katherine Scardino, his Houston lawyer who helped secure his release.

I finally got to hug Dewayne after eight long years of working on his case. Bethany Benitez, Chris Tate, and Megan Whisler all came to see Dewayne.

I love Kiearra like my own child. I promised I would return her father back to her. She is a beautiful and smart young lady.

Casey Kaplan with Dewayne before a presentation at the University of Texas School of Law in Austin. Dewayne would not be a free man without Casey's dedication and passion. Casey and I are forever "brothers in Brown."

"Team Brown" reunited for the Texas Defender Service Awards luncheon in October 2015. From left is me, Bethany Benitez, Dewayne, Casey Kaplan, and Megan Whisler. Dave Case from K&L Gates attended the lunch, but is not pictured. I am grateful to Dave for asking me to work on Dewayne's case.

I surprised Dewayne in Austin with a trip to a tattoo parlor to get these to signify our brotherhood. Dewayne's has the number 154 as he is the 154th exoneree from death row in the United States.

Dewayne and my wife, Anna, after a presentation at the place where I met Anna—the Catholic University of America Columbus School of Law. The law school was very supportive and invited me to speak about Dewayne's case several times. Anna gave me the strength and courage to keep up the fight for Dewayne, and I am forever grateful for her support and love.

Dewayne is enjoying his freedom and is living a quiet, peaceful life.

PART IV:

The Fight for Dewayne's Life

Chapter 23:

In Praise of NOBs

The NOBs are the good men and women of the "Noblesse Oblige Bar." They are the pro bono partisans of justice working out of elite law firms in New York, Washington, Chicago, San Francisco, and other major cities. These firms typically represent top-collar corporate clients but also take on, without charge, some of the most difficult pro bono cases, including death penalty cases. In these cases, which can take many years, they invest considerable billable hours and money.

The NOBs believe in doing well and in doing good. In their corporate work, they charge their well-heeled clients some of the highest rates known to mankind, including over $1,000 per hour. In their death penalty work, they defend the condemned at no charge. They embody the honorable belief that good fortune in life comes with an obligation to help others.

The NOBs haunt the corridors of all major law firms in this country. Some firms employ full-time pro bono partners who screen and take on important work. Some have foundations to support the firm's charitable giving efforts, with tens of millions of dollars donated each year.

They do good and meaningful work, taking on various types of cases: from immigration cases, to representing victims of domestic violence, to civil rights cases, Guantanamo Bay detainee representation, and protecting the integrity of elections. All of this for the greater good, and for no fees.

The cynics say the NOBs only crusade against the sin of capital punishment to expiate their far greater sins of defending rapacious corporations, union-busting management, and Wall Street speculators. But I am not cynical about the NOBs. I was one of them. Without the Noblesse Oblige Bar, I would have never gotten Dewayne's case.

But I would also learn the limits of the Noblesse Oblige Bar in a very personal way.

Chapter 24:

Life-Changing Phone Call

"You want to work on a death penalty case?"

It was March 2007. I was an associate at K&L Gates in the Washington, D.C., office. I started working at the firm in 2004 as an associate after I left the public defender's office in New York. Anna and I had recently had our first child, Ella, and we simply could not live on two government salaries any longer. Anna was a prosecutor for the District Attorney's Office in New York, a very prestigious job. She did her job ethically and never let the immense power prosecutors wield go to her head. But with our two small salaries in New York and the new costs for daycare or a nanny, we just couldn't make it work. We moved from a tiny one-bedroom apartment on the Upper East Side (we had been in a 350–square foot studio apartment in Alphabet City prior to the one-bedroom) to Alexandria, Virginia, so we could start our suburban life.

I worked in the securities enforcement practice group of the firm, which meant I was working on civil and criminal cases typically arising out of investigations by the Justice Department, the Securities and Exchange Commission, and FINRA. We were very busy, and I worked with a good group of young attorneys I enjoyed working with.

One day I got a call from Dave Case, a senior litigation partner in the D.C. office. Dave is a soft-spoken and wise old-school attorney who rolled up his sleeves every day and worked hard with no fanfare. Even though he worked at a large law firm and later became the Managing Partner of the D.C. office, he dressed plainly and drove an old American car. I respected Dave and wanted to impress him.

"You want to work on a death penalty case?"

Without hesitation, I accepted. The case was *State of Texas v. Alfred Dewayne Brown.*

Chapter 25:

The Appeal Process

A person convicted of a capital offense in Texas can file a "direct appeal," which is an appeal to the Court of Criminal Appeals in Austin, Texas, where you can challenge the conduct of the trial. You can raise issues about jury selection, the venue, evidentiary rulings by the judge, and whether the evidence before the court was sufficient for a conviction. These are arguments based on the "four corners" of the trial transcript. If it happened at trial, it can be objected to. This is not typically a fruitful avenue for death row inmates, but they are routinely filed as a matter of course.

In Dewayne's case, the court appointed a man named Charles Hinton as his counsel for his direct appeal. Hinton was a former district attorney in Harris County and had been a defense lawyer for more than twenty years by the time he worked on Dewayne's case.

On December 4, 2006, Hinton filed an appellate brief, challenging several things, including a challenge to the legal sufficiency of the conviction based on the accomplice corroboration rule, alleging that Shon's testimony was not sufficiently corroborated by independent evidence. The appeal also challenged a jury selection issue known as a "jury shuffle," in which a defendant's attorney can ask that the court "shuffle" the jury, or essentially start from the middle or back of the prospective panel of jurors rather than the front. These requests are made when there is an insufficient sampling of people in a particular part of the pool, such as all white people or all men in the first one hundred of the pool.

Another challenge was to some comments made by Rizzo in his closing argument, in which he called Loretta Muldrow "sleazy" and a liar. These types of personal attacks are not allowed in a closing argument, where the prosecutor is supposed to stick to the facts of the case and make arguments about those facts.

On September 24, 2008, the Texas Court of Criminal Appeals affirmed Dewayne's conviction. Significantly, the Court highlighted Ericka Dockery's testimony as critical corroboration to Glaspie. The Court also noted the testimony of Lisa Hubbard, Sheikh Mohammed Afzal, Sharonda Simon, and the telephone records introduced into evidence.

The Court also reprimanded Rizzo, stating that his response was improper and "was not tailored to the facts in the record or to misstatements of opposing counsel," and "delved into matters that were well outside the record." But that did not justify overturning the conviction and granting a new trial because "the certainty of conviction absent the misconduct [by Rizzo] remains unchanged."

The court's lecture to Rizzo, stating unequivocally that he made improper arguments, did nothing for Dewayne. It didn't give him any relief or a new trial.

Chapter 26:

The Writ

Aside from the direct appeal, the primary avenue for a defendant on death row to challenge his conviction is a writ of habeas corpus. The writ, which in Latin means "we command that you have the body," was established by the Magna Carta in 1215 and was essentially an early precursor to the Due Process Clause of the Constitution.

The writ is a way to have a defendant challenge his conviction and his sentence based on anything that has happened before, during, or after his trial. The main things that are raised are newly discovered evidence, like DNA testing and affidavits from witnesses who may have come forward late or changed their stories, and "ineffective assistance of counsel," which is a claim that a defendant's constitutional rights were violated because his or her defense counsel did not provide a legally sufficient defense. The writ is also where you can provide additional evidence of intellectual disability or new punishment evidence. This is a very shorthand version of what a writ is, but it is basically a "kitchen sink" way for defendants to put forth any and all final claims that they should not be on death row and should not be executed.

The writ process is very long and time-consuming. The process begins in the state court by filing a brief with the same judge who presided over the trial. This stage is critical because a defendant is in a "use it or lose it" stage. If you don't make your claims in state court, you most likely have waived them forever.

The state trial judge will issue a recommendation on whether relief should be granted, and sends it to the Court of Criminal Appeals. The Court of Criminal Appeals makes a determination, typically adopting the trial court's recommendation. If relief is denied, then the defendant can seek review from the United States Supreme Court. If that is denied, then the defendant goes from state court to federal court, or United States District Court for the Southern District of Texas in Houston, where claims are made again, this time before a federal judge who has no background on the case and who has to largely defer to the decisions made by the state courts. By law, the defendant has to file that petition in federal court within one year. That federal judge makes a decision, and if relief is denied, a defendant can appeal to the United States Court of Appeals for the Fifth Circuit in New Orleans, where that Court reviews the findings of the United States District Court. If relief is still denied, then the defendant can petition to the United States Supreme Court again.

Tired yet? Now that is the process if only one petition is filed. There are what is called "successive petitions" if something new arises after the initial petition is denied, and the defendant wants to file it with the court—more appellate rights potentially come with those filings. There are other types of remedies such as seeking clemency from the governor. So, when you hear about death row inmates accused of tying up the court system with the appellate process, it is usually in reference to the writ process.

The writ part of the case was what we were asked to do.

Chapter 27:

The Team

"You are in for a big one here."

We needed to quickly assemble a team to get to work. The initial inquiry about taking Dewayne's case came from Texas Defender Service in Austin. They are an amazing nonprofit group of activists who seek out NOBs to take on death penalty cases and offer support during the process. The first thing they did was hook us up with Mandy Welch, a living legend in the death penalty bar. She and her husband, Dick Burr, represented Timothy McVeigh in his death penalty appeals. Mandy was paid by the federal court to counsel and advise attorneys handling death penalty cases, particularly the NOBs, because the well-intentioned big-firm lawyers who always wanted to work on such cases did not usually have the experience or the knowledge about the process.

"You are in for a big one here," she said the first time we talked. She said this was a high-profile case in Houston because it involved a policeman on the verge of retirement, and a defenseless store clerk on her first day back to work after a maternity leave. She said that Dewayne's trial attorneys did a very poor job. We had a "big bell to unring," she said.

Mandy also hooked us up with Richard Reyna, a death penalty investigator who worked on a number of high-profile cases in Texas. She assured us that no one would be better to track witnesses down and get to the bottom of the case. He was a former sheriff in a county outside of Houston, and was ready to start knocking on doors.

As far as attorneys, Dave asked me to take a leadership role on the case, and I was all too happy to do so. We also needed an attorney in the firm's Dallas office, because they were licensed in Texas and I was not. Part of the advantage of being in a large firm like K&L Gates is that there are offices in every corner of the U.S.

and the world. We were referred to Lin Medlin, an appellate specialist, who was going to help write the brief on the case and assist us with local Texas practice.

We also got the help of junior associate Bethany Nikfar, who was a journalist prior to becoming a lawyer and thus passionate about tracking down good stories. In her short time at the firm, she had already worked on another Texas death penalty appeal.

Later on in the case we added Chris Tate, a hard-working, crazy-smart associate who, to this day, is among the most talented young lawyers I have ever worked with. I also liked that he had blue-collar roots like me. He grew up in Pittsburgh and was hungry and willing to hustle. Chris would take on a task and always do it perfectly. He, like me, also seemed to live on Diet Coke and adrenaline alone, a perfect associate for a death penalty case.

Bethany and Chris were passionate in their support of Dewayne's case, unwavering in their desire to get him justice, and willing to do absolutely whatever it took to get the job done. In fact, at Chris's wedding, one of the prayers was for all those who were wrongly imprisoned, which I thought was cool. We also enlisted the help of paralegal Craig Gaver, who is now an attorney in part because of the dedication he saw from me, Bethany, and Chris. The team was set. Two veterans of the Texas death penalty bar, one senior appellate specialist, a couple of junior associates who were well-intentioned but green, a paralegal, and yours truly—also well-intentioned and also very green. It was my first case defending someone sentenced to die.

Chapter 28:

Meeting Dewayne

"I didn't do what they said I did."

I was driving a green Mustang convertible, top down at top speed, heading north on Route 59 from Houston. I was heading toward Livingston, where Dewayne Brown was incarcerated in the Polunsky Unit. I was about to meet him for the first time, and feeling very fortunate to be on the case. With me was Lin Medlin, who was feeling very hot with the top down and who forced me to stop for sunglasses and a NASCAR hat from a dollar store in Splendora.

We picked up Mandy Welch for lunch. You could tell right away she was a true believer. "You ready for this? Gonna take a ton of work," she said. When we got to the visitor's gate at the prison, a guard in a cowboy hat made us get out of the car, open the hood (one time I visited and a guard asked me to open the hood, so I asked him to check the oil, and he actually laughed), open the trunk, the glove compartment, and the middle console. After we were cleared, we parked the car and walked to the front entrance. We went through a metal detector, and had to take off our shoes and belts. We were not allowed to bring in anything but legal papers, car keys, our driver's licenses, and two rolls of quarters so we could buy Dewayne food from the vending machines.

After we passed through the metal detector, we walked about three feet to the front gate control room. A guard sat behind a desk in the room that was enclosed with a thick sheet of glass, and smiled at us. "First time?" she asked. I cracked a small smile and nodded.

We walked into the main reception area of the prison. A friendly woman came and escorted us to a back office, the inmate records office, where we signed our names again in a large registry book and wrote who we were going to see and for what purpose. "Alfred Brown—Legal," I wrote. A large nouveau Christian mural extended across the entire wall of the room, with a double strand of a crown of thorns roped around the entire top part of the rectangular room as if we were all under the thorns. It was odd, especially for a state-owned facility. As if the Supreme Being had decided to visit the inmate records room and pass judgment on the out-of-town lawyers coming in to sign and see their condemned clients. It did not feel as welcoming as my home parish in Jersey.

I walked down a corridor past a barber shop for the non-death row inmates, a small room where they held church services, and display cases with jewelry made by inmates for people to purchase. I saw a Betty Boop belt buckle and a large glass sculpture in the shape of Texas. Texas art was everywhere. The inmates had tremendous pride in the state that condemned them.

The death row visiting area was very similar to other visiting areas of other prisons I had been to. In the middle of the room was an enclosed row of about twenty-five to thirty individual cells for the inmates. There were two chairs in front of each of the stalls, and small ledges for the visitors, all of which were carved into with various forms of graffiti. A large sheet of glass separated the inmates from the visitors. There were telephones in the stall for the inmate and one for the visitor on their side of the stall. There was a separate, enclosed attorney visiting room away from the general visiting area with two chairs and two phones. It is the same setup as the general visiting area, but with more privacy because you could shut the door. There were no contact visits on death row, not even for lawyers. All communications were done by crappy phones through which you could barely hear.

There was a sign above one of the doors to the visiting area. It said, "Do the Right Thing." I thought of Spike Lee and Chuck D and tapped my chest.

Dewayne was brought to us about fifteen minutes after we got there. He was exactly what I pictured him to be: big but not threatening, with an easy, almost sweet smile. I told him we would work very hard for him, and he thanked us. I asked him what happened that day.

He told us his story. It was simple. He was asleep at his girlfriend's house on the day of the murders, and he did not shoot anybody. He didn't have much else to say about his case. "I didn't do what they said I did," he said. That was it. I believed him. I felt a shot right to my heart. My inner tuning fork went off like a siren. Holy shit, I thought instantly.

That night we stayed in a hotel in downtown Houston. I was in Room 910. When I walked into the room, I opened the blinds to survey downtown Houston. I had a splendid view—the brightly lit and imposing headquarters of the Houston Police Department. I went down to the lobby to meet Lin for dinner, and there were two police officers watching television. I felt for a moment like they were watching me.

The next day we visited Dewayne again to talk more about the case. He seemed depressed. He said that he was frustrated to be on death row for something he didn't do. He said that he tried to recall anything about that day to help us, but he didn't remember much except that he was home. He seemed to start to cry for a second, and then composed himself. We reassured him that we were working hard for him and would give him the best possible shot in court. He seemed inconsolable.

I put my hand up to the glass to say goodbye and do a "jail five," and he barely put his up to the glass and didn't look at me when he did. We left the prison and flew back to Baltimore. I flew in and out of Baltimore even though it was far from my home in Alexandria, because the flights were cheaper out of there and I had told the firm I would keep the expenses under control. I felt terrible the whole drive home, internalizing the pain that Dewayne was feeling.

When I got home after my first visit, I was very emotional. I had a very hard time sleeping because I was thinking about Dewayne constantly. I woke up and prayed and cried. My oldest daughter Ella, who was almost three at the time, asked me where I had been. I told her I visited Dewayne in prison. She asked me who Dewayne was, and I said Dewayne was put in "time-out" for doing something he didn't do. Ella quickly stated, "Daddy, that's not fair." I hugged her, said that I agreed, and that that was why I was trying to get him out of time-out. I said it was going to be very hard, but I was going to keep trying because, as we say in our house all the time, "never give up." Ella drew a picture for me to take to Dewayne, a picture of a smiling sun. When she handed it to me, she said, "Daddy, you are brave. Tell Dewayne to be brave, too."

On my next trip to Houston, on August 13, 2007, we reviewed the state's file on the case. Working with us was Richard Reyna, the investigator. At lunch, Richard told us about "old Houston," when he worked as an investigator for the Sheriff's Office. He would take a fifty-dollar bill and tear it in half, and give it to a witness. If the witness brought back the information he wanted, the witness would get the other half. We told him we were willing to get as many fifties as he needed for this case. He said he wanted to focus on finding and interviewing Ericka Dockery, as we all agreed she was the most critical witness.

We got through thirteen boxes in two days, reviewing everything in the file, including police reports, photos, and witness statements. It didn't take long to find something that was interesting, maybe even disturbing. In his criminal trial, Dashan Glaspie had been represented by a defense attorney named Alvin Nunnery. Other documents in the file showed that Nunnery was Loretta Muldrow's law partner. We were surprised, even shocked. Ethical rules prohibit attorneys in the same firm from representing conflicting interests. As for two lawyers from the same firm defending a murder suspect and the chief prosecution witness, it is hard to think of a bigger conflict of interest.

While we were working, Rizzo stopped by the conference room. When I mentioned we were working on the Brown case, he affected not to recall the man he sentenced to death. "Which one was that again?" he asked smugly. I was not impressed by him or his cavalier attitude. I was about to tell him we were going to kick his ass in court and walk Dewayne out one day. Instead I smiled and shook his hand.

The next day we went to visit Dewayne. It was an execution day at Polunsky. We couldn't use the attorney visiting room because lawyers for Kenneth Ray Parr were meeting with their client for the last time. Parr was set to be executed for the rape and murder of a mother of two in her trailer in Bay City, Texas. Parr was eighteen years old at the time. Now twenty-seven, he was about to die. The attorney visiting room was filled with Parr's family members, religious people, and his attorneys, who were frantically running in and out of the room in vain hopes of a last-minute respite. We had to cut our visit short.

As I left the building, I came very close to throwing up. I had just seen what would happen if we didn't succeed. Dewayne would die. I vowed that day to do all that I could to make sure I would never be frantically running around as Dewayne was prepared for execution.

Parr was executed by lethal injection that evening.

Chapter 29:

The Third Guy

"Dobbie that wasn't nothing but one big set up for you."

As we pursued Dewayne's appeal, I kept picturing the crime unfolding at the ACE Cash Express store, and I kept asking myself and others, "Who was the third guy?" Everyone agreed that three men were involved in the robbery and no one disputed that two of them were Shon and Ghetto. Based on Shon's account, Rizzo claimed that Dewayne was the third man. The jury agreed. I was sure they were wrong, but I couldn't prove it because I didn't know who the third man was.

The initial logical choice, based on the testimony at trial, was Ernest Matthews, a.k.a. "Deuce." Several witnesses placed him at the VA on the morning of the robbery. He had a long criminal history of (1) possession with the intent to deliver a controlled substance; (2) manufacturing and delivering a controlled substance; (3) resisting arrest involving a police officer; (4) unlawfully carrying a weapon; (5) possession of marijuana; (6) possession of a controlled substance; and (7) murder, in 1995. On paper, at least, he looked like a more likely armed robber than Dewayne, who had only the one misdemeanor possession of PCP conviction.

I asked Loretta Muldrow if Deuce was the third man. She said no, but offered no thoughts of her own. It turned out she had not devoted much time to thinking about this central question of Dewayne's defense. Her time sheets showed only a half hour of work on the question of "Deuce v. Doby." Morrow also billed a half hour to "review rap sheet for Ernest Matthews." That was it. My initial thought was that Deuce was the third guy, but I was far from sure.

We met with Dewayne and then went to see his brother, A.B. Brown. He was a few years older than Dewayne and we heard from some folks that A.B. basically sold drugs for a living and lived a street life. We suspected that A.B. knew something about the crime of April 3, 2003, but had not come forward. In jail for a drug distribution charge, A.B. agreed to talk with us. He said that Ghetto slept at his house on the night before the robbery. He did not recall seeing Dewayne on the morning of the robbery, and did not recall him coming to his house to get a jacket, as Shon testified at trial. He did not believe that Dewayne was capable of such an act. He said he did not have any idea who the third person was.

There was something about A.B.'s performance that didn't sit right with me. Maybe it was my BS meter. He always responded correctly, with a "sir" or a "ma'am," but it felt fake and calculating. We sensed he wanted to protect Ghetto and his brothers of the streets more than his own flesh and blood brother.

On the flight home to Washington, I started reviewing the documents we gathered from Muldrow's file. One was a handwritten letter from May 20, 2003, just over a month after the incident. Dewayne had received it in jail, and given it to Robert Morrow during a court appearance. Dewayne could not read the letter himself because he didn't know how to read, so he trusted his lawyer to read it. When I got to the end of the letter, I wanted them to turn the plane around and take me right back to Houston. What was in the letter? Only what actually happened on April 3, 2003.

The letter to Dewayne came from a person named "Smooth," who I later figured out was a man named Jesse Coleman. He wrote that he had an encounter with a person named "E.W." in May 2003. Smooth recounted that he had gone to E.W.'s house to buy marijuana, and they started talking about the robbery at the ACE Cash Express store. E.W. said, "That day, that shit was crazy, I thought them boys was going to give me up." E.W. proceeded to tell Smooth about the fateful day he spent with Shon and Ghetto.

The crime went down like this, according to the letter: Shon picked up E.W. that morning, and was trying to reach Ghetto. Shon initially dialed the wrong number and called Dewayne. E.W. said that Shon said, "My bad, Doby, I called the wrong number," and said that Dewayne sounded "half asleep." They went to A.B.'s house to pick up Ghetto, and they were going to "hit one or two stores like we normally do and chill the rest of the day." E.W. then stated that Ghetto told them that they needed to "hit that ACE check-cashing place, 'cause it don't be no laws [police] there." They could "hit this place and go back to the hood."

They pulled up to the furniture store, discussing how they were going to do it. They saw a man standing in front of the furniture store smoking. Shon said to go into the furniture store, and so E.W. and Shon went in. When they came out, Ghetto was already in the ACE store, and E.W. and Shon joined him.

The letter continued:

> Shune [Shon] and E.W. joined T [Ghetto] inside the ACE store. E.W. said that Shune was holding the girl while T was going through stuff. E.W. said he was at the front door watching out, and before he knew anything a police pulled up, so when E.W. saw the law, E.W. ran to the back and said it's a law outside, Shune said shit, T what we going to do. T ran to the door, shot, E.W. said he looked back and saw Shune shoot the girl. E.W. said he ran to the car and Shune and T came behind him. They went to the VA. E.W. went to Nikki [Colar]'s house to wash his hands, and then went to the "big girl house." They all left the VA, and Shon's girlfriend picked him up from the VA.

The letter ended: "Dobbie that wasn't nothing but one big set up for you."

Holy shit. Oh, my God. I read it a couple more times. "Dobbie that wasn't nothing but one big set up for you."

So who the hell was E.W.?

Chapter 30:

Lost Letter

I remembered that there was a witness statement with a guy with those initials, so I ripped through the files I had on the plane. There it was, Elroi Walters. He was a friend of Ghetto and Shon's who was currently serving a five-year sentence for armed robbery with a gun. E.W. may have been the third guy we had been looking for.

Where had this letter been? It was in the bottom of a U.S. Postal Service box that Nunnery gave me from Muldrow's file, basically gathering dust. I almost didn't even copy it because it was at the bottom of the pile and looked like Muldrow hadn't even read it. In other words, Muldrow and Morrow had a road map to the crime the whole time and didn't do much of anything with it. Even worse, Dewayne couldn't read, so he had the best piece of evidence in his hands and he couldn't decipher it.

What Morrow did do was forward the letter to their investigator to speak with Dewayne about it. It seemed like Morrow's intentions were good at the beginning. "Please go to the jail and see Dewayne as soon as possible and review this letter with him," he told the investigator. "After that it is my intention to have you seek these people out and attempt to get sworn statements from them." Sadly, this never happened.

The investigative notes related to the letter are dated November 13, 2003, over five months after the letter was given to the investigator. The notes show that the investigator assigned to the case spoke to Dewayne about the letter. Dewayne identified the people who are referred to in the letter, including E.W. Dewayne told the investigator that he didn't know E.W.'s full name, but he heard that he was involved in a different robbery case. Dewayne also told the investigator that E.W. looked similar to him, same complexion but with more facial hair. The notes state "end of interview . . . " a few pages later, and that was the end of the work done on this letter.

From my experience as a public defender, I can tell you that handwritten letters from jail are usually suspect. But in a death penalty case with little forensic evidence and not all that many clues, this one should have been followed up on. The interview should not have ended the investigation; it should have been the beginning of unraveling the case against Dewayne, but it wasn't.

Chapter 31:

Protecting E.W.

The facts of Jesse Coleman's letter appeared to check out. Critically, they were facts that were not in the media or the public as of the date of the letter, so they had to come from someone with knowledge of the incident. Picking up Ghetto from A.B.'s house, the furniture store owner outside smoking, the facts of the shooting were consistent with the ballistics reports, where they went in the VA afterwards, and how Shon was picked up by his girlfriend. All accurate facts relayed by someone who knew what actually happened.

Smooth also stated that he went to see E.W. at his house because E.W. "can't leave the house." In fact, E.W. was on house arrest in May 2003 (he was not on house arrest on April 3, 2003, however) with home monitoring by an agreement with none other than Dan Rizzo of the Harris County DA's office. Also, Smooth and Shon had spoken that day, when Shon called him and said that the clerk had to die because she "got out of line."

We looked for other evidence in the DA's file that would have connected E.W. to the crime if they hadn't been so focused on Dewayne. E.W.'s mother, Betty Walters, told a Houston Police Detective that she had seen all about the robbery and murder on the news and that Ghetto called her house on the day of the robbery to tell her son that they had to get rid of a gun:

"Allen (the HPD Detective) advised Ms. Walters that we were aware that one or two of them had called her son, E.W., on the date of the double murder, and we were interested in what her son knew about it. Ms. Walters stated she was standing right there when the call came in and she thought her son was talking to a person he calls as [sic] Ghetto. Ms. Walters stated the caller said something about being in trouble and they had gone back to the apartments and something about getting rid of the gun."

When approached by police, E.W. declined to give them permission to search his room. In subsequent communications with the police, E.W. acknowledged knowing something of the potential "inside girl" at the ACE location who could assist in the robbery. It was clear that E.W. was intimately familiar with the facts of the incident and the people involved. E.W. also had a criminal record, including an aggravated robbery with a deadly weapon for which he received a five-year sentence. E.W. also had prior convictions for possession of marijuana, and a felony for delivery of cocaine when he was seventeen years old.

Finally, E.W. sent a letter to Shon while they were in jail that was revealing. He wrote that he had heard that Ghetto was going to try to implicate Shon in the crime. He instructed Shon to "hold your head because they shot shit at you from every angle they can think of, hoping you'll crack. . . . But remember your hand is the best, so hold your head, it'll be alright."

E.W. lamented that they should be playing football rather than being in jail. "I feeling sick right now because I supposed to be running the ball for T.S.U. (Texas Southern University) right now, not wearing this bullshit orange," he wrote. I was beginning to see a theme not unlike the movie *Boyz n the Hood*, where the gangsters try to protect the guy who has the football scholarship, but ultimately the ghetto life wins. Maybe E.W. was their shining hope for better lives, so they went along with Rizzo's desire to blame Dewayne instead. He wasn't going anywhere in life and was easy to get one over on.

Was that plausible? We would find out. I could not have been more jacked up.

Chapter 32:

Witnesses Recant

"They kept telling me that I could be arrested and lose my children if I kept saying that I couldn't identify Dewayne inside the Grand Am."

Richard Reyna had progress to report. He informed me that he met with Lisa Hubbard, the woman who said she saw Dewayne at the VA on the morning of the incident. She provided an affidavit stating that her trial testimony was incorrect, and that she was pressured by Rizzo to give her false statement.

Hubbard stated she did not read her statement in which she refers to Dewayne being involved in the incident, and her new affidavit stated that her statement about Dewayne "is not true." She said that she signed her original witness statement under duress. I have italicized the key statements of her affidavit:

> About one or two weeks before the trial of Dewayne Brown my sister and I met with some of the homicide detectives, Mr. Rizzo with the District Attorney's Office and a female who was with Mr. Rizzo. I was able to read my statements. I told them that "Doby" had nothing to do with the crime.
>
> *Mr. Rizzo told me that if I didn't stick to my statements, they could charge me with perjury.* The female with Mr. Rizzo then told me that not only would they charge me with perjury but that they would also charge me with theft of the $10,000 that Crime Stoppers gave me. I was frightened and I did not want to go to jail but I insisted to all of them that Doby had nothing to do with the shooting of the woman and the police officer.
>
> *When I testified at Doby's trial I substituted Doby for Deuce because I thought that this is what Mr. Rizzo wanted me to do.* I also did it because I did not want to be arrested even though I would be telling

the truth. If Doby's lawyers would have tried to talk to me before the trial I would have told them the truth but no one ever came around even though I was still living in the same apartment.

Our case was starting to come together. A main witness who testified that she saw Dewayne at the VA on the morning of the incident did so under pressure by the DA and the police. Now she was saying she never actually saw Dewayne that day.

Reyna had more. He had also obtained an affidavit from Sharonda Simon, in which she stated that she could not actually identify Dewayne as the man in the Grand Am at the VA on the morning of the incident. She said she met with Rizzo, and told him the car was *more than the length of a football field away from her.* She was told by Rizzo not to mention how far away she was. "It looked like it could have been Doby because I just assumed that it was him because everyone else was out there that morning," she said in the affidavit. She testified as she did because she "felt pressured and frightened" and did not want to go to jail and lose her children.

The pressure was real. She said that "prior to the trial I was visited several times by the detectives and they kept telling me that I could be arrested and lose my children if I kept saying that I couldn't identify Dewayne inside the Grand Am." But, she said, "The truth is that I was never able to identify Dewayne Brown as the man sitting inside the white Grand Am."

The sad reality was that all people living in the conditions of the VA had levers that the police and the DA could push: cash rewards, probation, parole, jail, and, of course, child and family services. The easy lever to push on Sharonda was her kids. Of course she didn't want to lose them, and she wanted the police and DA out of her hair, so she gave the DA what he wanted. Now she had recanted, too.

Chapter 33:

The Brief

With information on a third suspect and two recantations, we had plenty of information to file in our writ. We worked on the writ on airplanes to and from Houston. We worked in hotel suites set up like war rooms with gallons of caffeinated drinks and all kinds of junk food scattered about. We worked at home after the kids went to bed and during the workdays in between projects for paying clients. We were fully aware that the writ was the most critical document for getting Dewayne off death row.

The final brief was a whopping 258 pages, by far the longest brief I had ever worked on and likely will ever write. We made a legal claim that Dewayne was innocent of the crime. We claimed that Muldrow provided ineffective assistance of counsel. We challenged the way Rizzo pressured Lisa Hubbard and Sharonda Simon, and how he badgered Ericka Dockery in the grand jury. We also objected to Dr. Denkowski's very questionable methods.

The day before it was due, we pulled an all-nighter. We hit the Burger King across the street from the office for some late night fuel. We finished at about 5:30 a.m. Our paralegal Craig Gaver flew with the writ to Houston to file it. He got into an accident on the way to the airport. He survived, and so did the writ, and it was filed on time.

With the writ filed, all was quiet on the case for about a month. I had to attend to other business for the firm. My billable hours were way off because of the sheer volume of time it took us to do the writ. I wanted to show the firm that I was dedicated to both pro bono pursuits and to the billable work that paid for those pursuits. But I missed the action of working on Dewayne's case.

Chapter 34:

Another Letter

"I know he doesn't belong here."
"Why?"
"Because he wasn't there."

In March 2008, my colleague Bethany Nikfar received a letter at her office in Washington, D.C.

"Ms. Bethany. Hello. How are you doing? Well my name is Elijah Joubert. I'm quite sure you already know who I am, so I really don't have to explain who I am. But I just want you to know that I'm giving you my personal consent that you can come and seek me out and talk to me about any legal matters you want. I don't care what my lawyers say, I'm only looking out for my friend, that's my only concern."

The suddenly chatty Ghetto had something to tell us. Bethany and I, working on another case in Miami at the time, were excited about the development. We confirmed with his lawyer that we were planning to visit his client. On March 27, 2008, Bethany and I went to Houston and drove up to Livingston.

Before the meeting with Ghetto, I did something I can honestly say I never thought I would do. I caused a flood on death row. We were waiting for them to bring Joubert to the room, and I went to the bathroom. It was an old bathroom, with a very creaky sink, a toilet that looked like it was from 1920, and a very small, rectangular, blue prison-issued bar of soap. I washed my hands and turned the hot water knob off, but it wouldn't shut all the way off. I turned it on and off again, but it still ran.

I looked at the knob quizzically, and decided to try one more time, but with a little more force. It didn't work. The knob came off! Water shot up like a geyser from the hole where the knob used to be, and I got drenched with water. I put my hands over the hole but I only got wetter. I quickly shut the door and came out soaking wet. The water started to come out from under the door crack, and pretty soon the whole visiting area was under a couple inches of water.

People who were visiting got up on the shelves of their visiting stalls to avoid the water. It caused quite a commotion. A plumber eventually showed up and shut the water off. Some non-death row inmates came by with paper towels (which made me laugh because of the volume of water), mops, and a wet vac.

I got a standing ovation from the death row inmates as they all laughed themselves silly. I bowed several times. When I came for future visits, the guards told me not to use the restroom while I was there.

The guards finally brought Ghetto into the visiting room once we dried off. He certainly lived up to his nickname. He had a mouth full of gold teeth and a body covered in tattoos. He was all street.

"The fuck you want, man?" he greeted us.

I said that I was trying to get Dewayne off the row because he didn't belong there. He sat back, playing coy.

"I know he doesn't belong here."

"Why?"

"Because he wasn't there."

I felt a smooth rush of emotion in me as his gold teeth-filled mouth smirked at me.

"Then who did it?"

"I ain't no snitch, motherfucker," he said. "I will say your boy wasn't there, but I won't say who was." He explained that he lived with "morals and principles."

"Fair enough, man," I said. I told him that I used to be a public defender in Brooklyn, so I understood the code of the streets. I repeated I was simply trying to help an innocent man get off of death row. I wanted his help on the third guy involved in the robbery and murders.

"If I say who I think it is," I ventured, "will you tell me?"

He agreed. I leaned forward, almost pressing my face to the glass. I wanted to look at him straight in the eye.

"Was it E.W.?"

He paused, slouched way down in his chair. He looked to his left and to his right. He straightened up, leaned in, touched his nose, and looked me in the eye.

"How the fuck you know that shit, man?"

I told him about the letter. I mentioned my initial suspicions of Deuce. Ghetto said that Deuce was a hustler, or a drug dealer, but not a jacker like Shon and E.W. He paused again, looked back and forth to see if anyone was looking.

"OK, man, here it is."

Chapter 35:

Ghetto Comes Clean

"You guys have done a great job pursuing this."

Ghetto then told us how the crime really went down, and this time he was mostly telling the truth.

He said he had gone with E.W. and Shon to the first check-cashing place to rob it. When the manager flashed his gun, they backed off. They went to the VA to regroup.

Then they went to the ACE Cash Express store. When they got there, E.W. and Shon went to the furniture store, and when the woman came to ACE, E.W. jumped her. Shon went in behind him. A couple minutes later the cop came, and E.W. shot him. Ghetto said that he didn't go into the store; he was the getaway driver.

After they sped away, they went to the VA to Nikki Colar's house, and then Shon and Ghetto made one last stop at Shondo's. After Shondo's, they went their separate ways.

He explained that he and Shon had protected E.W. because he had a football scholarship to Texas Southern University, and he was going to play in the NFL and take care of all of his boys. Ghetto was also close to E.W.'s mother, and didn't want to get him involved. He said that E.W. and Ghetto did many "scores" together. He then said that E.W. and Shon were reckless and did a lot of robbing together. E.W. also sold drugs with Shon. Ghetto and Shon were tighter with E.W. than they were with Dewayne.

When he finished his story, I felt numb. I always felt Dewayne was innocent, and I had a feeling that E.W. was the guy, but the way Ghetto told the story, I knew 100 percent that Dewayne was not the guy.

Even though we were bubbling over with optimism regarding the case, and ready to shout it out for all to hear, we didn't even have a court date set for a hearing on the brief we filed. We knew we were in the early stages, and that was hard to accept because I wanted it over with. Right then. No waiting. Done. Now. Right goddamn then. But I knew there was a process we had to follow, and we didn't want to seem above the process as a bunch of pushy, Yankee lawyers. We understood why we had to let certain things run their course, but we didn't like it at all.

I emailed Dave Case when we got back from the Ghetto meeting to update him, to thank him for taking the case on, and for the opportunity to work on it.

"You guys have done a great job pursuing this," he said.

Chapter 36:

Uncle Mo

That's about when the case started going stale. I am a big believer in momentum. It probably comes from my love of sports. I played two years of college basketball (don't be too impressed, I scored all of four points in those two years on the JV squad) and played basketball and baseball, my two favorite sports, in high school. I have watched hundreds of sporting events, and in games like basketball, baseball, and football, momentum, or "Uncle Mo," was critical. I felt like Uncle Mo had left the building for a long time on Dewayne's case. The case file was on the back of my desk as I worked on other cases. We heard nothing from the DA or the judge.

But Uncle Mo came back. We secured an affidavit from Ghetto on our next trip to Houston. He was less confrontational than at our first meeting and still willing to help. He signed a one-page affidavit that included the statement: "*Alfred Dewayne Brown was not involved in any way with the incident on April 3, 2003, nor present at the ACE check-cashing store on April 3, 2003.*" Welcome back, Uncle Mo.

Chapter 37:

The Problem of Elected Judges

"God wanted me to keep my job."

One challenge we faced was Texas's system of elected judges. In August 2008, we had a video status conference with Judge Ellis and Inger Hampton, the district attorney who was assigned to respond to our writ.

Judge Ellis thanked us for the hard work on the very thorough writ. He said he would order the trial lawyers, Loretta Muldrow and Robert Morrow, to write an affidavit in response to our writ to get their perspective. After the affidavits were filed, Judge Ellis said, we could narrow down the issues and have an evidentiary hearing.

There was one potential complication, he added. He was up for reelection in November. He said that if he lost, he would clear his schedule to get us a hearing before the end of the year so he could give the case the benefit of his knowledge. His opponent was not very experienced, he said. It would not be good for the bench and bar if she were elected, he continued.

His opponent, Mekesha Murray, was a Democrat, which sounded good to me. But this was South Texas, so Murray vocally favored the death penalty, plus she was married to a cop. I thought it was virtually impossible that, if elected, she would free a man convicted of killing a law enforcement officer. I jokingly told Judge Ellis I would send a campaign contribution.

All kidding aside, the exchange illustrated why elected judges are a deeply problematic feature of death penalty justice. With an election coming, Judge Ellis had every incentive to delay hearing Dewayne's appeal. Any fair judicial action he took in the case could—and surely would—be portrayed by his Democratic opponent as a favor to a "cop killer," proof he was "soft on crime." By doing his job in the courtroom, Judge Ellis might well ensure that he would lose it at the polling place.

Now multiply Judge Ellis by thousands of judges—thirty-nine states have some form of elected judges for trial courts—and you have the dimensions of a problem that is headed for the U.S. Supreme Court. Elected judges are, by any measure, far less likely to reverse death penalty verdicts than appointed judges. A Reuters investigation of thousands of capital punishment cases heard in thirty-seven state courts over the last fifteen years found a strong correlation between the results in those cases and the way each state chooses its justices. "In the fifteen states where high court judges are directly elected, justices rejected the death sentence in 11 percent of appeals, less than half the 26 percent reversal rate in the seven states where justices are appointed," wrote reporters Dan Levine and Kristina Cooke.

As Justice John Paul Stevens wrote in 1996, "Persons who undertake the task of administering justice impartially should not be required—indeed, they should not be permitted—to finance campaigns or to curry the favor of voters by making predictions or promises about how they will decide cases before they have heard any evidence or argument. A campaign promise to 'be tough on crime,' or to 'enforce the death penalty,' is evidence of bias that should disqualify a candidate from sitting in criminal cases."

The threat to judicial independence—and thus to justice—is obvious. Consider the case of Justice Penny White, who was the only woman on Tennessee's Supreme Court. In the early 1990s, she had served for two years on the state's appellate court and confirmed the overwhelming number of criminal convictions that she reviewed. In 1994, Democratic governor Ned McWherter appointed her to the state's highest court.

In the first death penalty case, she joined the unanimous vote of the other justices in affirming the conviction of Richard Odom for rape and murder but overturning his death sentence. She also joined, but did not write, a three-judge majority opinion in the same case, which found insufficient evidence to uphold Odom's death sentence under Tennessee's capital punishment law.

Two years later, in the judicial election of August 1996, the Tennessee Conservative Union attacked her as an opponent of the death penalty. Her opponents, including the state's Republican leaders, accused her of never voting "to uphold a death penalty conviction," even though Odom's appeal was her first capital case and she had upheld his conviction. They accused her of wanting to "free more and more criminals and laugh at their victims."

Both of the state's U.S. senators voted absentee before the official election and publicly announced that they had voted against Justice White because of her decision in this one case. The Republican Governor, Don Sundquist, proclaimed before the election that he would never name someone to a criminal court judge-ship unless he was sure the nominee supported the death penalty. White was prohibited by the rules of judicial conduct from discussing the Odom case and defending her legal position. In the end, she lost the election.

If she had violated her sworn duty to follow the law and voted instead to execute Richard Odom, she would have kept her job.

While elected judges can appeal to popular passion in the short term, they do damage to the credibility of death penalty justice in the long term, as the sorry example of Alabama shows. Alabama is one of four states allowing elected trial judges to override jury verdicts of life and impose death sentences at their own discretion. Since 1976, Alabama judges have overridden jury verdicts *111 times.* Although judges have authority to override life or death verdicts, in 91 percent of overrides, elected judges have overruled jury verdicts of life to impose the death penalty.

By 2013, nearly 20 percent of the people currently on Alabama's death row were sentenced to death through judicial override, according to a study done by the Equal Justice Initiative, a criminal justice reform group based in Montgomery.

Judicial override "is the primary reason why Alabama has the highest per cap-ita death sentencing rate and execution rate in the country," the study concluded. "In 2009, with a state population of 4.5 million people, Alabama imposed more new death sentences than Texas, with a population of 24 million."

In November 2013, the Supreme Court declined to hear a challenge to Alabama's judicial override. In a fifteen-page dissent to the court's decision not to hear the case, Justice Sonia Sotomayor declared that there is only one rea-son, supported by empirical evidence, why Alabama uses the judicial override, whereas other states have moved away from the arbitrary practice: judicial poli-tics. "Alabama judges, who are elected in partisan proceedings, appear to have succumbed to electoral pressures," she wrote with the concurrence of Justice Stephen Breyer. Sotomayor cited the examples of several judges who imposed death penalty overrides on multiple occasions after having campaigned on sup-port for capital punishment. One judge cited the murderers he has sentenced to death in a campaign ad. Another admitted in a 2011 news report that voter reaction does "have some impact" on sentencing decisions, "especially in high-profile cases."

Sotomayor called on the court to consider the strong possibility that the impact of death sentences on electoral politics constitutes "cruel and unusual punishment" under the Eight Amendment. At the very least, she wrote, the prac-tice "casts a cloud of illegitimacy over the criminal justice system."

Without comment, Justice Scalia voted with the majority to refuse to hear the case. But avoiding the issue in Washington doesn't change the reality of American courtrooms and prisons. The cloud of illegitimacy created by elected justices is another reason why the death penalty is dying in America and has to change.

When Election Day came, Democratic candidate Barack Obama ran strong in Harris County. Farther down the electoral ticket, Democrats won twenty-three of twenty-seven judicial races. Some Republican judges who had twenty-five years of experience were defeated. Of the four Republican judges who survived, one was Judge Ellis in the 351st Judicial District of Houston.

"God wanted me to keep my job," Ellis told the *Houston Chronicle*, adding that, "I'm glad I won and glad I have four more years to work for the county. I hope and pray their [the experienced judges who lost] replacements do a good job."

I hoped that God was going to tell Judge Ellis to let Dewayne out.

Chapter 38:

The Trouble With NOBs

"HOLD!!"

In 2009, I became fatigued by the case. Maybe all of us had underestimated the amount of time and effort that it was going to take. If it was a DNA case, I would probably have already gotten Dewayne out, and the firm would have been very excited to have taken on the case and been a part of righting an injustice and would have received the appropriate amount of favorable publicity. However, now I felt, and I suspected the firm felt as well, that we were in for much more time and effort with a very uncertain result at the end.

I was learning the limits of the Noblesse Oblige Bar. I was learning that the NOBs, no matter how qualified and dedicated and idealistic, cannot single-handedly solve the problems of the death penalty jurisprudence.

It was a difficult experience, personally and professionally. I was working on other cases, but I kept thinking about Dewayne and how we needed more and more. I was stricken with self-doubt and wondered whether I would be sitting at his execution, kicking myself for not finding something new we hadn't found before, and being mocked by some of the attorneys in my office who didn't want to take the case in the first place and who thought it was a waste of precious resources and time. I tried to keep such thoughts out of my head, but as days went by and we didn't have any new developments, I became increasingly pessimistic. Was I foolish for agreeing to take this? Were the personal and professional sacrifices simply too great?

I was seriously going crazy inside. There was always a strong strain in me that brought me back to the feeling that Dewayne was innocent, and I should hold tight and keep fighting. I would recall Russell Crowe's heroic stand in the movie *Gladiator*. Facing an army of chariots, he circled his fellow gladiators and screamed "Hold!!" I would tell myself under my breath, and sometimes loudly in the car on commutes home from work: "Hold." I was trying to hold as best I could, but I never felt as cool or as strong as Russell Crowe.

So, in November 2009, I took a trip to Houston to try to make my own luck. I wanted a new investigator to work on the case, to take a fresh look. Suzette Ermler, who helped us when the writ was filed, was willing to get involved but hadn't really started yet, so we decided to take a couple days to take matters in our own hands and do some investigation of our own.

I flew out of Baltimore again. Ironically, while I was in the security line, I saw a former partner at K&L Gates whom I respected. When I told him I was going to Houston for my death penalty case, he chuckled. The firm did not care at all about pro bono work, he said. "Stop what you are doing now, or you may not be there for much longer. Be very careful."

I realized that I was spending two days away from the office, two days that I could be billing clients my $500 per hour rate instead. I hoped he was wrong about the firm, but I didn't want to press my luck.

Chapter 39:

Death Row

"Listen to me. I WILL get you out of here. I promise you."

As I was driving on a back road through a thick, hazy Houston on my way to the prison in Livingston, I was again overcome with a deep sense of pessimism about the case. The newly reelected judge had put us on the back burner, and I had very little to report to Dewayne. I felt like the mountain was just too damn big to climb. Then came a divine intervention. I tuned to a Christian radio station, and suddenly the holy melody of "Amazing Grace" filled the car. *How sweet the sound.* I sang along, cried, and I shook off the mental fog I was driving in. I also thought of my mother, who died of lung cancer in 2008. Her friends told me that towards the end of her cancer, my mother asked them to save their prayers for her and to pray for Dewayne to be released instead, because she knew how important his case was to me.

Once I got to the prison and met with Dewayne, my doubts were wiped away. His youthful innocence, not unlike my children at the time, reminded me why I was defending him. He brought me something I had not had in a long time—peace. The man who was in solitary confinement gave me comfort and hope. I was immediately refocused and centered. I told him I would be filing some DNA motions. He showed me three drawings of sports cars that he traced from a magazine. He had artistic talent, and was proud of his work.

He said he had talked to a guy on his unit about where he would go if he got out. He said he would go back to Louisiana with his daughter, Kiearra. He told me that he missed her a lot and thought about her every day. I told him I would buy him a house so he could be with her. He became quiet, and clearly emotional, not quite crying, but as close as I think I ever saw from him.

I stared right at him. I put my face very close to the glass and put my hand on it and banged against it. I said, "Listen to me. I WILL get you out of here. I promise you. I know you didn't do it, man." He looked up, eked out a very small smile, but then put his head back into his hands. I kept my hand on the glass. He looked up after a few seconds and said, "I didn't do it. I would put everything I love on it, and I don't love much." He put his head down. I cried and repeated my promise and told him to get his hand on the glass. He finally put his hand up to mine.

We then eased up the seriousness of the conversation. I went and bought him some food. He told me that a guy on the unit made some hooch out of orange juice and peaches and butterscotch, and got drunk and hooted and hollered all night. Dewayne thought it was funny. We laughed like old friends.

I felt his pain as a father, so I made sure that on that trip I went to see Kiearra myself. I met her at the VA where her mother, Sharonda, lived with four other kids, including one with cerebral palsy who was confined to a wheelchair and a feeding tube. I did some homework with Kiearra, a Lewis & Clark worksheet, and took her to the corner store run by a couple of fearful Asian men behind bulletproof glass. I let her pick out whatever she wanted, and to her credit she made sure she got something for each of her siblings and her mother. As we walked back I took her hand and said to her, "I will do my best to bring your Daddy back to you." She smiled and hugged me tightly and then ran off to her apartment to show her siblings the goodies we bought.

Despite my promises, our investigation was stalled. Ericka Dockery was elusive. When Suzette finally found her, she cursed her out, yelled at her, and refused to cooperate. We wrote letters explaining we were trying to help Dewayne. She didn't respond. We had various addresses for her—for one of them I literally dove into the trash can that was at the curb to see if I could find a piece of her mail, if she actually lived there.

We asked the judge to order a series of DNA and fingerprints tests to see if E.W. had been at the crime scene. The results came back and we struck out on every one. The clothes had too many mixed DNA profiles to make a database comparison. The fingerprints did not come back with a hit. A fingernail scraping from Alfredia Jones came back with only her DNA. The good news was that none of the DNA came back to Dewayne. The bad news was that we simply did not have a forensic case.

I didn't share all of that with Dewayne, but I did tell him that we could not locate Ericka, and he was upset about that. He still couldn't understand why she testified the way she did at trial, when she knew the truth about what happened that morning. He was depressed.

We were seated in the general visiting area because it was another execution day. Dewayne said that one of his fellow prisoners, Cowboy, had just received a stay of execution. Another prisoner, Ozone, had just been executed. A third prisoner Dewayne called "Cuban Cubano" was to be executed that day. Cuban Cubano was in the attorney visiting room having his picture taken with his family. In less than twelve hours, his life would be extinguished by the state of Texas. It was surreal, and it made me sick. I looked at Dewayne and I motioned towards Cuban and said, "That will NEVER happen to you. Never." I don't think he felt reassured. And I was not sure I was going to be able to make good on my promises.

Chapter 40:

Unringing the Bell

"I felt the Houston detectives and the grand jury wanted me to change my story because they kept pressuring me and harassing me to get my times right with the times they wanted to hear."

The end of 2009 was slow for Dewayne's case, but not for me personally. My wife gave birth to our third child, Andrew Henry, born on December 1, which also happened to be our eighth wedding anniversary. I was excited to have a son, and I named him after my father and my grandfather. My family was complete. I remember crying almost uncontrollably as the doctor, who is a bit of a wiseass, told me to look up to see what we had. She showed me a little bag of peanuts.

In April 2010, we finally caught a break thanks to the hard work of Bethany and Suzette. They went to Houston to meet Reginald Jones, Ericka's cousin, who was at her house on the morning of April 3, 2003. We always thought he was a critical witness. All the while Dewayne had told us he was home that day, and Reginald was a way to prove that.

Reginald had a very good recollection of the events, and also brought up a theme we had heard before: pressure from the police and Rizzo. He signed a four-page affidavit stating, "Alfred Dewayne Brown was home with me on the morning of April 3, 2003, at my cousin Ericka Dockery's apartment." He stated that he was playing video games and watching TV on the couch in the living room of the apartment from 9:00 a.m. to 11:00 a.m. He said that he saw Dewayne come downstairs into the living room sometime between 10:00 a.m. and 11:00 a.m. Based on the layout of Ericka's apartment, Reginald explained that he "could see the front door and the back door from the living room couch where I was sitting." He concluded, "Dewayne did not walk through these doors on April 3, 2003."

Reginald also stated that his initial witness statements were not completely accurate, in part because he felt pressure to cooperate with police who told him what to say. "I felt the Houston detectives and the grand jury wanted me to change my story because they kept pressuring me and harassing me to get my times right with the times they wanted to hear," he declared.

This was a huge development. We knew from reviewing schematics of Ericka's apartment that based on the layout, Reginald would have been able to see who entered and left the apartment on the morning of the incident. He said that he saw Dewayne come downstairs between 10:00 and 11:00 a.m. Dewayne had not gone out and he had not returned. He was, as he said all along, at home that morning.

When I read the affidavit I was excited, but also angry that Loretta Muldrow had not put Reginald on the witness stand during Dewayne's trial. She had suggested to the jury that Dewayne was at home that day—after of course she had argued that he was "merely present"—but then gave them no reason to believe it.

I wrote a letter to Inger Hampton at the district attorney's office to inform her of the new affidavit. I hoped she would take the information seriously. I hoped she would interview Reginald himself. I hoped she realized we had a legitimate and real innocence claim in this case, even if we didn't have a DNA case. I dared hope that we might unring the bell.

Chapter 41:

Code of the Streets

"I am not your attorney. Your attorney knows why we are here. I am Doby's attorney. Let's get to business."

On August 6, 2010, Bethany emailed me the startling news that Elroi Walters had just been arrested for murder. According to a news account, the incident occurred in March 2009. The victim, John Doe, "stepped out of his car after parking it on the side of the street in front of the Braeburn Colony apartments where he lived when another man. [Walters] walked toward him and the two exchanged words. The man pulled out a gun and shot Doe. He took a white plastic bag that belonged to Doe and then sped away in a red, newer model Toyota Camry."

So, E.W. got out of jail in May 2008 for an armed robbery, and then ten months later, he killed someone. John Doe should still be alive.

The first thing I wanted to do was call the *Houston Chronicle* and tell them that we told the DA and the Court in April 2008 that Elroi Walters, a potential suspect in the ACE Cash Express murders, was about to be released, and we were ignored. Now, ten months later, he had killed someone over an argument over a "white bag," which I am sure did not contain gummy bears. After some discussion with colleagues, I settled on a more measured approach. We provided the DA's office with the information about E.W.'s potential role in the ACE Cash Express murders and demanded that they conduct a full and thorough investigation.

Inger assured me that she would put a flag on Walters's file, so that his case would not be disposed of without notifying her. She said she knew that we had been talking about Walters for a long time. "Why are y'all so high on him?" she asked.

I told her that we would bring our best case to her. Remarkably, she said that if we were able to make our case against Walters, she would do what she could to exonerate Dewayne.

I wanted to see Ghetto again. With Walters in jail and likely to stay there for a very long time with this new murder charge, maybe he would abandon his "code of the streets" in favor of telling the truth. I contacted his attorney, a solo practitioner named Kurt Wentz, and asked if we could speak with Ghetto. We met at the prison in Livingston.

Kurt was an affable guy who had been beat down by the Houston criminal justice system. When we talked prior to Ghetto's arrival, it was clear to me that the deck was stacked against Kurt. He got $25,000 per writ, and that included funds for experts and investigators, leaving little for his own services. We had spent well more than one million dollars on legal fees, investigators, psychologists, psychiatrists, and other experts in Dewayne's defense. Kurt had 2.5 percent of that amount. He didn't have a lot of hope for Ghetto's case. Given the high-profile nature of the conviction, and the lack of good legal issues in his case, Kurt said that relief was unlikely. He also said that he did not want to push this case through the courts too fast because he would only be accelerating an execution clock. He said we could speak with Ghetto for as long as we wanted.

Ghetto came in to the visiting room, picked up the telephone, and started yelling at Kurt.

"You ain't done shit for me, and now you come by because Doby's lawyers want to speak wit' me? You a piece of shit, man."

Kurt told Ghetto to listen to what we had to say.

"Get the fuck out of here, man," Ghetto said. Kurt was glad to oblige him. He went to visit another client who was on death row.

"What the fuck do you want?" Ghetto glared at me.

"We are here because your boy E.W. was arrested for murder."

He went from pissed to interested to skeptical and back to pissed in the course of a few seconds.

"The fuck you talkin' bout, man?"

I said that it was time for Ghetto to go on the record and say what really happened in this case. I said Walters was facing a long prison term, maybe even death.

"Fuck you, man."

Ghetto didn't want to be seen as a snitch. He would be looking over his shoulder the whole time in prison if he did that. He had a "code of ethics" to uphold, he said.

"Your code is shit," I told him, suddenly angry. "You willing to die for it?"

I explained that he was on the road to execution. He could either shut up and die or listen to me and do the right thing.

"I don't give a damn about you," I said, pounding my fist on the glass. "I am not your attorney. Your attorney knows why we are here. I am Doby's attorney. Let's get to business."

It was the ghetto hustler against the Jersey guy. I credit my father for the courage to stand up to this guy. He never took any shit from anyone and was made of iron. He taught me street sense and toughness and never to back down from a fight. This fight was a little different though. Who was going to blink first?

I got up and went to the vending machine to buy a soda and a chicken sandwich. When I came back, I was still hot. I said, "You want to leave? Go the hell back, I'll eat your goddamn chicken sandwich. I am hungry."

I started packing up my stuff and walked towards the door.

He finally got the hint. He tapped lightly on the glass. I shrugged my shoulders and flipped my hand up as if to ask him what he wanted. "I'll stay," he smirked. "Talk to me, man."

I went over how the truth could help Dewayne, and how Kurt could try to use this new information to help his case. He said that he had a nine-year-old daughter, and asked if we would set up a trust fund for her. He was a hustler until the end. I said we would do no such thing. I advised him to work with his lawyer. There would be no deals between us at all. Just tell the truth.

He agreed to talk with the district attorney.

Chapter 42:

The Case Restated

We then gathered all the information we had on Walters. We wrote a nine-page letter with fourteen exhibits, arguing that Walters was the third man at the scene of the crime. We supplied the history of the case, our prior interest in Walters, and then provided evidence for Inger to consider. We sent the letter from Smooth with a detailed recitation of why it was a real letter. We argued that the facts showed that Walters, Shon, Ghetto, and A.B. were all friends and all partners in crime.

When Inger got the package, she gave us a call. She had just returned from maternity leave after giving birth to twins. She was "very appreciative," and said that it was very helpful to "connect the dots" in this case. "I am the last person on earth who wants an innocent man on Death Row," she said.

She was not adversarial in her tone. We hung up ecstatic and almost without words. She was saying all the right things, and she now had the evidence in a neat package. Were we getting closer or was Inger paying us southern lip service?

Chapter 43:

Anthony Graves to the Rescue

"I know what you went through. Talk with us, please."

Ericka Dockery. Her name resonated in my mind. I spoke it aloud hundreds of times. "Ericka, Ericka, why can't we find you? Why can't we speak with you?"

I knew that without Ericka, and now likely no DNA, an innocence claim would be very difficult. I actually gave up ever finding her or talking with her, and then it happened. Suzette called us and told us that she had gone to Ericka's house once more to speak with her. Desperate and running out of options, she brought along some help, a man named Anthony Graves. He had spent eighteen years in the same prison where Dewayne was held before being exonerated just hours before his scheduled execution. I knew about his case, and knew that he was working as an investigator for the Texas Defender Service. I thought it was cool that Graves dedicated his life of freedom to investigating other cases. I was not sure what he could do for the case when Suzette first mentioned him to me, but I was happy to have such a high-profile person on the case.

Graves had been arrested for a particularly heinous murder of a family of six in Somerville, Texas. Like Dewayne's case, there was no physical evidence linking him to the crime. The main witness against Graves, Robert Carter, recanted in very dramatic fashion. Carter was literally on his deathbed in the Huntsville, Texas, death chamber when he was set to be executed, and he said, "It was me and me alone. Anthony Graves had nothing to do with it. I lied on him in Court."

After a very long and drawn-out legal battle that played out in Texas state and federal courts, Graves was given a new trial. The state could not retry him based on insufficient evidence, and Graves was released in October 2010.

On August 15, 2011, Suzette and Graves went to Ericka's apartment at approximately noon. They knocked on the door and one of Ericka's daughters answered. Graves asked to speak with Ericka. She came to the door, saw Suzette's familiar face, and then she saw Graves. He said that he had been on death row and was set free because he was innocent. He said that he had a girlfriend who had been pressured by the prosecutors.

"I know what you went through," he said. "Talk with us, please."

Ericka asked Suzette if she had put Graves up to this. She said that Graves heard about Dewayne's story and volunteered to help. Ericka took a deep breath, opened the door, and invited them in.

"Tell the truth and don't be afraid," Graves said. Ericka started talking. She said that she and Dewayne were very close, and their lives were going pretty well when all of the events happened. One day she was helping him look for a job at Walmart. The next day he was arrested for the shooting. She said that she wanted to see him, look him in the eye, and talk.

She said part of the reason why she had avoided Suzette before was her husband at the time, Julius Lockett. He was very protective and Ericka did not want any reminders of her past knocking at her door. She and Julius separated after a while, and then they got divorced. He was convicted for selling drugs and went to jail.

"I had been praying on it, and thought if someone came back to talk to me, that I would," she said.

This was the break in the case I had been waiting for since 2007. Ericka was a critical witness and was so grateful that Suzette, with Anthony's help, had finally broken through. The initial interview was a good icebreaker, but we needed to know more on the key points that emerged in Dewayne's trial.

Then Ericka got a case of the proverbial cold feet again. She was hard to get in touch with and harder to pin down. She moved a lot. She lived with her sister Jeanette, who said she didn't want Ericka to speak with us, and told her not to sign anything. With every day I didn't hear something, I thought that Ericka was going to be gone forever. We had a chance, I thought, and we blew it.

Chapter 44:

"I Am Troy Davis"

"This court has never held that the Constitution forbids the execution of a convicted defendant who has had a full and fair trial but is later able to convince a habeas court that he is actually innocent." — *Antonin Scalia*

What made the Ericka waiting game worse was that on September 21, 2011, the state of Georgia executed Troy Davis. I sat in full attention to the live feed on CNN, and sat on my couch on the verge of being sick. I stood up, jumped up and down a few times, and paced back and forth. Troy Davis's case was very similar to Dewayne's. No forensics. No DNA. Just witnesses, and most of them had flipped and recanted.

Nevertheless, the state went through with the execution and likely killed an innocent man. I watched the crowd at the candlelight vigil wearing shirts that said, "I am Troy Davis." I heard the media reports that the Pope and Jimmy Carter pled for his life, and the European Union begged Georgia not to go forward with it. I watched Davis's very sad attorney address the media. The execution happened at 11:08 p.m. I stood up, stared at my TV, saying, "No, no, no" over again, and I cried.

Would I be there in ten years, addressing reporters about how an innocent man was executed? I felt absolutely terrible and feared the Texas machine of death might ultimately prevail in Dewayne's case.

One of the Supreme Court opinions in the Troy Davis case made me feel even worse. It came from, who else, Antonin Scalia. The justice issued another Scaliaism: *"This court has never held that the Constitution forbids the execution of a convicted defendant who has had a full and fair trial but is later able to convince a habeas court that he is actually innocent."*

Reread this pearl of wisdom a couple of times and ask yourself, what the bleep? The Constitution does not forbid the execution of an innocent man?

Come on. Really? I was appalled. I felt only marginally better when I read an article entitled "Scalia's Catholic Betrayal" by Alan Dershowitz, the Harvard Law School professor. He called Scalia's statement "shocking," and he singled out Scalia's oft-professed Catholic faith as the reason why. "Surely it is among the worst sins, under Catholic teaching, to kill an innocent human being intentionally," Dershowitz wrote. "Yet that is precisely what Scalia would authorize under his skewed view of the United States Constitution."

As a Catholic, I couldn't have agreed more. But that wouldn't mean a damn thing if Dewayne's case ever landed on Justice Scalia's desk, and it was my goal to make sure it never did.

Chapter 45:

Ericka's True Story

"Brian, no, he never said he was there."

After several more weeks of allowing self-doubt and remembering haunting images of Troy Davis, I got a call from Suzette that Ericka Dockery was finally ready to talk. Bethany was going to go, but she was pregnant and had a bad case of vertigo, so I said I would go. I got on the first plane I could. Along the way, I was having an out-of-body experience. Could it be that I was finally going to talk to the most important witness in the case? Would she tell me that Dewayne really was not at her home on the morning of the crime? What if she told me Dewayne really did admit to her that he was there at the crime scene?

Ericka was critical, because the Court of Criminal Appeals had ruled that her testimony corroborated Shon's story. If we were able to prove that her initial grand jury testimony was correct and her trial testimony was not, we could argue that Dewayne's conviction was legally insufficient under Texas law. We don't have to have DNA evidence. We don't have to have E.W.'s confession. All we would need to do is apply Texas law to the facts and show that the conviction could no longer stand.

We agreed that Suzette would pick up Ericka and we would meet for lunch at a local Cajun seafood place called Jimmy G's. I was in the parking lot at 2:30, looking at every car that came into the parking lot. Suzette called at 3:30 to say she was outside Ericka's house, but she was not there. I was convinced at that moment that I was going to have gumbo alone with Suzette that night.

Then Suzette called again.

"She's getting in the car, get a table."

I ran into the restaurant, asked for a quiet table in the back, ordered a sweet tea, sat and read the menu like six times, and went to the bathroom twice. All of a sudden, there they were.

What struck me right away was how beautiful Ericka Dockery was. She was short, maybe five foot four, with perfectly smooth hair, a light complexion, and a sweet smile with dimples. She was dressed conservatively in a pink sweater and black pants.

I had been thinking for four years about what I would say if I ever got the chance to talk with her, and all I could come up with was "Hi." What an opening line. She smiled and we ordered appetizers.

Suzette ordered boudin, which I had never eaten before. It looked like a sausage. Ericka laughed at me when I tried to pick it up and bite it. She passed me some crackers. "Use these," she said. She was very composed.

"Brian, what do you want to ask me?" she asked.

I told her I was sorry for all that she had been through. I said I didn't think Rizzo or the system treated her properly. I also apologized for all the times we tried to contact her at her home. She looked at Suzette and said, "She is very persistent." Suzette winked at her while slurping an oyster.

I told her I wasn't Rizzo. I said I had no power to put her in jail. I just wanted the truth, whether it was helpful or harmful to Dewayne.

My first question: Was Dewayne home when she left for work in the morning? She said yes. Before and during the trial, she said she had felt incredible pressure to say that he was not there when she left for work. She looked me in the eye. "Brian, he was there," she said.

She was calm and not the least bit intimidated. When she wanted to make a point, she put down her fork, and looked me in the eye. She was, in a word, believable.

My second question: Did she remember what the caller ID said when Dewayne called Alma Berry's house that morning.

"It was my house," she said. She recalled seeing her own phone number. She did not waver at all on that point. When I asked her about her trial testimony, in which she said that Dewayne was calling from "Shondo's" house, she felt embarrassed because she said she didn't remember saying that. She repeated that she remembered very clearly that the call had come from her house.

My third question: Had Dewayne threatened her before she went into the grand jury? Again, she looked right at me and said no. She said he never did.

My fourth and final question was the most important. I was shaking inside as I asked it. I was dying to know whether Dewayne actually said, "I was there," as she had testified at the trial.

I put down my pen and looked her right in the eye.

"Did Dewayne say he was there?"

I didn't ask in a confrontational way, more in a "I've just really wanted to know for four years."

"Brian, no," she said. He never said he was there. She said she had asked him one time, "All bullshit aside, were you there? Because I have to know." He said no. They both cried.

At that point I paused and tried to compose myself. I felt a kick under the table from Suzette.

"Do you feel better after telling us this?" Suzette asked.

Ericka said that she did, and said that she had not told anyone else this before. She had two reasons for coming forward, she said. First, she felt like a coward for not standing up and saying the truth before. She said she should have been strong enough to stand up and say that Rizzo was a bad man who made her say what she said. Second, she felt bad for what has happened to Dewayne. She understood that she had to make a choice between her kids and her future and Dewayne at the time of the trial, and she had to pick her kids. But, she felt she had some "bad ass karma" because of what she had done. She needed to make it right.

As we left the restaurant, Ericka asked, "What's next?"

I told her that if she was willing, I would like her to meet Inger Hampton at the DA's office. She said she would.

I asked her to sign a short affidavit. She agreed to do so without hesitation. I quickly scribbled some paragraphs on a piece of notebook paper. I read them back to her, and she signed.

Chapter 46:

The Affidavit

1.   My name is Ericka Jean Lockett. I am 36 years old and reside in Houston, Texas. I am the same Ericka Jean Lockett who provided witness statements to the Houston Police Department, testimony before the grand jury, and trial testimony in the prosecution of Alfred Dewayne Brown.

2.   The purpose of this affidavit is to state the truth about what happened in Dewayne's case.

3.   Regarding the telephone call from Dewayne to me at Alma Berry's house on April 3, 2003, I specifically recall looking at the caller ID device and seeing my home telephone number on the device. Dewayne said he was at my house when he called.

4.   Regarding my testimony at trial that Dewayne threatened me to tell the grand jury that he was home at 8:30 a.m. on April 3, 2003. Dewayne never threatened me about my testimony at the grand jury.

5.   Regarding my testimony that Dewayne said to me, "I was there, I was there," Dewayne did not say he was there. Dewayne always denied his involvement in the offense.

6.   I am coming forward now because I believe it is time to tell the truth about what happened.

7.   When I testified in the grand jury, ADA Dan Rizzo spoke to me in the room alone by the grand jury room. I was locked in the room. ADA Rizzo told me that he did not believe me, that I was not a good person, that he was going to take my children away by calling Child Protective Services, and that I was going to go to jail for a long time. I felt very threatened by ADA Rizzo throughout this whole case.

8.   For example, ADA Rizzo threatened me by saying that he was going to make me a co-defendant in the murder case, and I would never see my children again. At that moment, I was very scared and threatened by Mr. Rizzo. These threats are why I gave the testimony I did.

I swear this affidavit is true and correct.

Ericka Jean Dockery-Lockett
November 5, 2011

Years and years of work on the case, and it came to two quickly written hand-written pages of notes done in the front seat of a car. We left, and I shook Ericka's hand. I thanked her for coming, and promised to stay in touch.

I called Anna and cried. "She's telling the truth, buddy," I said. "Dewayne didn't do it."

"I knew it all along," she said.

Chapter 47:

Leaving the NOBs

We made plans to travel back to Houston for Ericka to meet with Inger. This was going to be a critical trip. It was also going to be a very meaningful trip for me personally, because this was going to be the last trip to Houston as an attorney for K&L Gates. I started at the firm in September 2004, when Ella was not even six months old, and by the time of the final trip to Houston, she was seven years old, and had a four-year-old sister and two-year-old brother.

The firm gave me a lot of opportunities and a significant amount of money over the seven years. We had enough money to buy decent cars, take nice vacations, and buy a nice home. I was able to work on some very high-profile cases, including the Senate Ethics Committee's Special Counsel investigation of former Senator John Ensign. I tried two federal criminal cases because the firm permitted me to take a reduced fee from the federal court to take the case on behalf of indigent defendants. I worked on a number of other meaningful pro bono cases from Catholic Charities for individuals who could not afford my fees.

I worked with some attorneys I respected. I met my assistant, Rayco Cheney, who was like a member of my family. I bonded with the guys in the mail room, including my friend John Thorpe, the most conscientious and loyal worker in the building, and my ladies in the catering department, who always let me know when a firm lunch was over so I could grab some leftovers and feed my Diet Coke habit. I am forever grateful for the firm, most especially for letting me work on Dewayne's case and never saying no to an expert, an investigator, or expenses for me to go to Houston.

But the firm changed while I was there. When I started, Kirkpatrick and Lockhart had about seven hundred lawyers. Named after two World War II veterans from Pittsburgh, the firm's humble roots are what initially attracted me. I did not want to work at a global mega-firm where you become a commoditized and institutionalized number rather than a person. But after several mergers,

Kirkpatrick and Lockhart became K&L Gates and ballooned to more than two thousand lawyers.

With that growth, the culture changed. Instead of a family-friendly place where there was an all-for-one and one-for-all attitude, where everyone looked out for each other and had each other's backs, the office felt cold and corporate. Everyone seemed to be looking out for his or her own individual interests and willing to stab you in the back to advance them. Our benefits were trimmed, and our health plan became worse and more expensive. The annual couple-thousand-dollar bonus the firm would put into our 401ks disappeared. Morale among the associates began to suffer. In a survey conducted by *The American Lawyer*, K&L Gates ranked forty-seventh out of fifty firms based on a number of topics such as firm culture, morale, compensation, partnership prospects, and commitment to pro bono work.

It felt like the cost-saving measures were all designed to improve the bottom line, which of course is a laudable goal if you are making quarterly earnings and have public shareholders, but when you are dealing with people, people you want to grow and develop into great lawyers and a great team, cost-cutting just kills morale and culture. It breeds a corporate mindset, a cold business, a place where the five minutes by the water cooler talking about your kids with a colleague cost the firm five minutes of billable time. Towards the end of my time there, a lot of people spent their whole day working with their doors closed.

I didn't get any bonuses while I was there, in part because only fifty hours of work on Dewayne's case each year counted towards the billable hour requirement for bonuses, and so hundreds of hours of my time per year were not counted and thus just wasted in the firm's eyes. Actually, Dave did manage to get the firm to give me a $2,000 bonus one year, because at bottom he is a good guy who recognized just how much work the case was taking. Other associates who did not do one hour of pro bono work received annual bonuses as high as $60,000. Some chided me and said I should drop the case so I could get those bonuses.

One associate, who is now a partner, told me that he/she was glad that I did so much pro bono work so he/she didn't have to. Another senior partner, prominent in the D.C. office, told me that he/she was very proud of the fact that he/she never did one hour of pro bono work and often bragged about that fact. There was a story about one partner who appeared in court for a pro bono case and scoffed at all the poor people. He said that his Mont Blanc pen was worth more than the life savings of most of the people in the courtroom.

But I noticed that the firm did not hesitate to put me in front of potential summer associates who were interviewing to tell them about Dewayne's case. The firm wanted me to be a "summer buddy" to the summer associates, mentoring them and giving them projects on Dewayne's case so they could see someone at the firm doing real-life meaningful pro bono work. In some ways I felt like I was being used, but I didn't want to lose the opportunity to work on Dewayne's case.

In 2010, the firm gave me the job title "Of Counsel." That same year, attorneys my age or younger were made partner. One of them was the person who said that he/she was glad that I did all the pro bono work so he/she didn't have to. It was no secret around the office that the head of the firm had once said publicly that that "Of Counsel" was a "disfavored title," and one that no one in the firm should strive to achieve. It indicated, he said, that the attorney didn't have what it took to make partner. When I was given the title, some of my friends called me "Mr. Disfavored." I laughed, but the joke was clearly on me. My career was beginning to suffer.

I didn't seek out Dewayne's case, it came to me from the firm, and now I was being penalized for the very case the firm asked me to work on. I made a commitment to the firm, and they responded to that commitment with actions that told me I should leave. I didn't want a parade or awards or even recognition for the work, I just wanted not to feel so vulnerable and marginalized by my own colleagues and by the firm itself for the work I was doing—and on a case they had given me.

It became clear to me that K&L Gates simply should have taken a pass on Dewayne's case. Maybe it wasn't the kind of NOB I thought it was. It also became clear to me that the firm didn't, or couldn't, because of the economics of the firm, care about me as a person the way I thought they did in 2004, and that was enough for me. It was over.

When I told Dave I was leaving, he thanked me for the work on Dewayne's case. He acknowledged that I was in a "precarious" position at the firm, so he understood why I had to leave. I was trying to save Dewayne's life, but in the process, I was potentially jeopardizing my own career. It was an almost-suicidal mission for me that was beginning to feel really dangerous for me and my young family.

And that is the problem with the NOBs, or at least this one. The profit-making law firm will almost inevitably treat pro bono death penalty cases as a form of charity, high-minded and worthy perhaps, but not central to the institutional mission. In a pinch, providing justice for someone like Dewayne was not a priority, and anyone who acted like it was would pay a price for his convictions. Such a conflicted profession cannot be counted on to fix the dysfunctional death penalty system.

I started to look for work and found a small firm that wanted me to take over the work of a partner who was going to retire in two years. "We want you here long term, and we want you to succeed, and are willing to do anything for that goal," said the managing partner who recruited me. It sounded like a solid opportunity, and I was glad. I knew I could not stay at K&L Gates any longer.

But the firm could not take on the burden of a long and costly death penalty case. I would like to say I was torn up about the decision, but it was not a very hard decision in the end. I had to be thankful and grateful for the work I did on Dewayne's case, and I had to turn it over to the most capable hands I could find. I would always help out on the case. All of this was on my mind as I flew to Houston on November 29, 2011. I took an early flight so I could connect and save the firm five hundred bucks.

Chapter 48:

Walk On

"Thank you for everything, man."

Once I arrived in Houston, I drove to Livingston, where I met up with Casey Kaplan, a fifth-year associate in the Dallas office. "Regardless of what happens down the road," he said to me in an email before we met, "you've got my commitment to see this thing through." That promise meant everything to me, as I knew Dewayne would be in smart, capable hands.

We had to wait an hour and a half for the visit because an inmate had acted up and the whole place was on lockdown. Finally, Dewayne came out. We talked about Ericka, and he seemed excited by the news that she was finally willing to come forward. He told us that he had recently seen his daughter and sister. He was happy to have seen Kiearra and talk with her about how she was doing. She got a very good report card, with all As and one B.

We bought him some food for what would be my final visit, so I had to make it good. I spent hundreds of dollars on vending machine food for him over the many times I visited him and I wanted the last one to be memorable. I bought him two cheeseburgers (one with bacon and one with jalapenos), two bags of pork rinds with Louisiana hot sauce, an apple, M&Ms, a Hershey bar with almonds, a chocolate pie, and two Sierra Mist sodas. It was an early Christmas dinner for him. He opened the bags very carefully, spread them out like a placemat, and separated each piece food by category (main course, dessert) and ate it all. He thanked us for the meal, and we talked about the case.

Watching him eat made me laugh, as I remembered one time that I was visiting him and we were running out of things to talk about, so I asked him one of my favorite questions of friends—what would be your death row meal? But then I forgot I was actually on death row. I said, "Sorry man, it's my job never to have you have a last meal here." He laughed and said, "No problem, man, crawfish."

At the end of the meeting, he asked me whether my kids liked the *Lion King*, because he was tracing a picture from the movie and wanted to send it to me. I thanked him and told him the kids would love it. Then I told him I was leaving the firm, and Casey would be taking over as his lead lawyer, but I would help Casey with whatever he needed on the case. He seemed a bit confused, but he and Casey got along during the meeting. I was happy about that.

"Thank you for everything, man," he said, and put his hands up to the glass. I put my hand there, left it there for a little longer than normal. I felt a small tremble in my hand. I stood up and said good-bye. I knew it wouldn't be the last time I saw him, but it would be the last time I would see him for a long time.

On the drive back to Houston, I was crying and listening to David Gray. "Slow Motion" was the song. I was lost in my mind and didn't see a car swerving into my lane on a very narrow road near an overpass. Casey was behind me in his car, and honked the horn to alert me and the other driver. The driver veered back into his lane, averting what would have been a very serious accident. Casey called me and said, "Dude, you have no idea how close that was." I thanked him for saving my life and agreeing to help save Dewayne's.

I woke up the next morning very peaceful. On my last day in Houston, I would bring Ericka Dockery to see Inger Hampton. Whether Inger's office would take the step of letting Dewayne go or whether we would soon have to schedule a hearing before Judge Ellis to put all of this before him, it was now time for action. I felt that I had done my best and then some. There was very little else to be done factually. I felt that years of work were ready to culminate in some long-deserved justice.

Suzette picked up Ericka and drove her to the courthouse. Even though she was moving to New Orleans to start a new job, she wanted to be there for this meeting with Inger. Her dedication was simply extraordinary. In her new job, she was going to do mitigation work for other death row inmates; those guys were lucky to have her. I am sure we would not have gotten as far as we did without her.

Before we went into the meeting, Ericka told me that she was not nervous because she was ready to tell what really happened. But I figured she had to be a little worried. The last time she talked to a DA, she ended up getting charged with perjury and wound up in jail until she told the prosecutors what they wanted to hear. I told her to do nothing more than tell the truth, good, bad, or otherwise.

We met in Inger's office. She started by giving Ericka a *Miranda* warning, telling her that anything she said there could be used against her in court and that she had the right to a lawyer. This put Ericka on the defensive. In my view, Inger was trying to rattle her. And it worked.

"Am I in trouble for coming here?" she asked.

Inger said that she couldn't answer that. When Ericka looked at me, I said to her that I couldn't advise her, either, because I was Dewayne's lawyer and not hers. She was free to talk or not to talk. All I said was, "Do what you feel is right." Ericka indicated she was ready to talk.

Inger began by asking open-ended questions like, "Why are you coming forward today?" and, "What do you want to tell me?" With such an opening, a lawyer or a sophisticated witness could start spinning their tale as they saw fit. Ericka did not know how to respond. She rambled a bit and looked jumpy. She said that she had been pressured to change her story by Rizzo, and she didn't want to lose her kids. Her testimony had weighed on her for years, she said. Dewayne should not be in jail for something he didn't do.

When Inger started asking questions in chronological order about the events of April 2003, Ericka was able to respond more clearly. She said that she and Dewayne had a fight the night before the incident, and she didn't want him to be with Shon and Ghetto because they were bad guys. Dewayne left that night and she went to sleep. The next morning, she saw him on the couch, and slapped him and said, "What are you doing here?" He laughed and rolled over on the couch. She got her kids ready for school and then either dropped them off at the bus or drove them, she couldn't remember, and then left for work. She recalled stopping at Burger King and buying Alma Berry a croissant sandwich.

Time was the central issue. Ericka said that she was asked multiple times by the police what time she left, and when she said she simply didn't know, she was told that that wasn't good enough. She had to come up with a time. Ericka maintained throughout the interview that she simply did not know. This showed me that Ericka was willing to say what she knew and nothing more. She wasn't willing to make anything up just to benefit Dewayne.

Did he participate in the robbery? she was asked.

"Well, he was sleeping at my house when I left, and then he called me from my house around ten." This was the phone call memorialized by the papers, which we didn't have at the time, residing in Officer Breck McDaniel's garage.

Looking back on that meeting knowing that the record was in their files makes me very mad, because Ericka was very sure about the call coming from her house. Ericka said that a call came to Alma Berry's house at around 10:00 that morning, and she heard Ms. Berry say it was from her house. Ericka recalled looking at the caller ID box, and it had her house number on it. She and Dewayne spoke, continuing their argument from the prior evening. Dewayne asked her to turn on the TV news about the shooting that had just happened.

When she got home from work that day, she said Dewayne was there. She took a nap and went to her second job. When people started calling the next day saying Dewayne was involved in the crime, Ericka told him to go to the police station and tell them where he was that morning. His mother and brother came by to take him to the police station. "You know what happened next," Ericka said.

Inger asked her about her grand jury testimony. Ericka said that she heard a lot of questions from grand jurors and felt immense pressure from Rizzo. During one break, she said that he had put her into a locked sitting area outside the grand jury room and told her that he did not believe her. He told her she was going to go to jail for a very long time. After that threat, she went back into the grand jury room and said that she could not recall what time she left that morning. After she testified, she said, she saw police officers hovering around her house every day. She felt harassed and threatened.

Ericka said that when she was brought back to court for a hearing on the perjury charges, Rizzo threatened her. "I am going to make you a co-defendant in the murder case," he said. Ericka said she was shocked and scared. She was willing to do whatever it took to get out of jail, regardless of what she had to say.

Inger then reviewed the statement where she said that Dewayne had threatened her and told her to lie to the grand jury and said of the crime scene, "I was there."

"Dewayne did not threaten me," she said without hesitation. "He never said he was there." She said she only made those statements because she wanted to make her testimony sound better to the DA. She was scared of what would happen to her and her kids if she didn't. She said she had asked Dewayne many times if he was involved in the robbery/shooting, and that he denied it every time.

The meeting ended with Ericka saying that she prayed for the victims' families and that she felt it was finally time to come forward.

While Ericka and Suzette went out into the hallway, I stayed behind to tell Inger that she had a game-changer on her hands. She had a good poker face, but I had interacted with her enough that I sensed she agreed.

I then told her I was leaving K&L Gates and that Casey and Bethany would handle the case from here. She told me that she, too, had news. She was moving from the writ division to the trial division, so Dewayne's case would be transferred to another writ prosecutor, probably Lynn Hardaway.

I then said that if her office was not willing to release Dewayne based on this new evidence, we wanted to get a hearing with Judge Ellis in the spring or summer of 2012 to put all of the new evidence on the record. Inger said what I feared she would say: she didn't think her office would release Dewayne without exculpatory DNA evidence or some other new evidence, besides Ericka's recantation. With that caveat, she said she would help to get a hearing on the court calendar as soon as possible.

On the plane home, the music of David Gray, Seal, and Bono accompanied me back to D.C. to my wife, kids, and the next stage of my life and career. I knew that I had done all I could for Dewayne to get him to this point. I played "Walk On" by U2, a fitting way to move forward.

PART V:

Justice, At Last

Chapter 49:

Convergence

After I left direct day-to-day involvement in Dewayne's case, all of the factors that are undermining the American system of capital punishment converged. The result was that Dewayne ultimately went free. The process was agonizing, excessively complicated, and emotionally draining, but the logic and facts were relatively simple.

The pro-death penalty "expert" witness whose bias and bogus testimony convinced the jury that Dewayne did not have significant mental impairment and who gave him extra IQ points for being "nervous" was exposed, fined, and disqualified from ever working on a death penalty case again.

The garage evidence emerged that had been withheld by Rizzo in violation of *Brady*, exposing the fact that the state had the document that would have confirmed Dewayne's alibi, but did not disclose it. While there was no effort to hold Rizzo accountable for his misconduct, a new Harris County prosecution team reluctantly but honestly faced the new evidence.

The elected judge hearing the case acknowledged that Dewayne's trial did not do him justice. When he called for a new trial, another group of elected judges on the Court of Criminal Appeals ignored his recommendation and waited seventeen months—until after the next election—to concur with his findings.

Having resigned from the case, I no longer qualified as an NOB, but my friends and colleagues did an exemplary job in marshaling the overwhelming new evidence that would eventually secure Dewayne's release. It helped that the firm changed the policy for counting pro bono hours after I left and gave Casey Kaplan hour for hour credit for his work on Dewayne's case. Good for Casey, too late for me.

But few of us, NOBs or former NOBs, labored under the illusion that we had "made the system work." In the end, we obtained justice for one individual, Alfred Dewayne Brown. We knew we were fortunate to prevail in a deeply flawed system. More than a few other equally innocent people have not been so lucky, and more languish in prison waiting for someone to stand up for them.

Chapter 50:

The "Expert" Witness

"Dr. Denkowski takes clinical interpretation beyond the realm of reason."

The first flaw in the death penalty system exposed in Dewayne's exoneration was the myth of the expert witness.

From the start of the appeal, I had pressed on the court the issue of Dewayne's mental impairment as it was presented to the jury during the trial. Bethany Nikfar worked directly with prominent medical professionals who provided affidavits calling into question Dr. Denkowski's methods.

Dr. Gary Siperstein, founder and director of the Center for Social Development and Education at the University of Massachusetts, declared, "Dr. Denkowski's assertion that Dewayne's depression and anxiety suppressed his performance on the WAIS-III, or negatively impacted his scores on the performance subtests in particular, is unsupported. . . . Such an unprecedented act reflects a total lack of understanding of scoring procedures and interpretation . . ." Siperstein went on to say, "There is nothing in the literature to support Dr. Denkowski's manipulation of Dewayne's scores." He concluded that "Dr. Denkowski takes clinical interpretation beyond the realm of reason. It is my opinion that Dr. Denkowski's assessment in this case fell below the accepted standards of interpretation and practices."

Dr. Thomas Oakland, who co-authored the American Psychological Association's 2002 code of ethical principles and conduct, expressed similar frustration with Dr. Denkowski's methods in his affidavit.

"The elevation of his full scale IQ from sixty-eight to seventy-two to seventy-seven is unsupported. The methods he uses violate standardized procedures and thus make his revised data unusable. Fortunately, we are provided with Dewayne's unadjusted full scale score of sixty-eight, one that should be used as the best estimate of his intellectual ability.

"Dr. Denkowski's acknowledged use of clinical judgment to change the scores of a standardized test undermines the purpose of standardized measures," Oakland went on. "The profession of psychology has not developed standardized methods for making score adjustments on instruments that measure adaptive behavior based on whether skills were or were not taught. It is my professional opinion that such score adjustments are absolutely invalid."

We also obtained new testimony from Doctors Jim Patton and Dale Watson. At the trial, they testified that they were unable to reach an opinion on whether or not Dewayne had an intellectual disability because of a lack of evidence on the adaptive deficit prong of intellectual disability. When provided with new evidence that they did not previously have, Dr. Patton stated: "Dewayne meets the three criteria of the definition of mental retardation." Dr. Watson reached the same conclusion.

The court took our affidavits under advisement. I didn't press the issue unduly because I thought Dewayne's claim of innocence was more important. I wanted him out. I wanted to hug him and deliver him back to Kiearra.

In February 2009, the Texas State Board of Examiners of Psychologists sued Dr. Denkowski. I wish I could say I was surprised. The board alleged he had intentionally misused or abused psychological testing. Dewayne's name was mentioned in the complaint as one of the individuals whom Dr. Denkowski had assessed incorrectly. Dr. Denkowski, the Board said, had "intentionally deviated from the norms of scoring methodology presented in the test manual for the ABAS-II, creating his own scoring criteria and substituting his clinical judgment for the scoring criteria." This was a serious complaint, like when an attorney faces disbarment.

Dr. Denkowski fought the case initially for two years. Then on April 14, 2011, he settled with the Texas State Board of Examiners of Psychologists. He received a reprimand and a $5,500 fine based on his death row mental evaluation work. Dr. Denkowski did not admit to any wrongdoing. He agreed not to "accept any engagement to perform forensic psychological services in the evaluation of subjects for mental retardation or intellectual disability in criminal proceedings."

The settlement got national attention. Senator Rodney Ellis of Houston told the *New York Times*, "We cannot simply shrug our shoulders and sit by and watch while the state uses legal technicalities to execute these intellectually disabled men . . . especially on the word of someone who is no longer permitted to make these kinds of determinations."

The DA's office let Casey know that they would no longer stand by Dr. Denkowski's testimony in Dewayne's case. They wanted a new expert, Dr. Tim

Proctor, to examine Dewayne. If the new expert agreed with the findings of our experts, then Inger Hampton said she would agree to a stipulated set of facts, which would result in a new punishment phase. In other words, the court would reconsider the issue of whether Dewayne should be executed or get life in prison, but not the question of his guilt or innocence. That was progress, but no comfort to Dewayne.

Chapter 51:

The Conflicted Judge

"Would it be better to literally just clear the decks and start over again?"

A second flaw in American death penalty jurisprudence was revealed during an October 2012 hearing about Dewayne's intellectual disability. While hearing our arguments, Judge Ellis openly mused that it might simply be best to order a punishment phase without delay.

> The more I think about this case and the more I think about the situation that we find ourselves in at this point in time . . . I find myself feeling that—and I'm not trying to shirk my burden in any way, shape, or form. I know it's my job to do this stuff, but finding myself feeling that would it be better to literally just clear the decks and start over again?
>
> Does it make sense to go through potentially years more of litigating the writ or does it make more sense to clear the decks and try this again and not have to worry about Dr. Denkowski and what happened with that in this particular case?

That was a heck of a loaded question, but he didn't answer it. Instead, he scheduled another hearing. Then politics intervened, as it inevitably does in those jurisdictions where judges are elected. A few weeks after Judge Ellis called for another hearing on the issue, he won another reelection in the 351st Judicial District. On November 8, 2012, he edged Mack McInnis, a Democrat, by a 51–49 percent margin. In an election where more than one million people voted, Ellis won by twenty thousand votes.

I never questioned Judge Ellis's integrity. Mostly he was a religiously conservative straight shooter, and he was conscientious. Some people may ask how could

Judge Ellis do justice in a death penalty case without thinking about the impact of his rulings on his chances of winning reelection and maintaining his livelihood. I prefer to ask a different question: how would I do justice in that situation? What if *I* wore the robes, and my livelihood and job were on the line when I made decisions in a courtroom? I think it would be very difficult for me to make dispassionate judgments, which is why I don't think judges should be elected. An elected judge is a conflicted judge.

All the same, I was glad Judge Ellis was reelected. He knew the case and, as the facts emerged, I could see that he wanted to do the right thing. We were lucky he would continue to preside. But his election was a reminder of the forces beyond the courtroom—beyond the facts of the case—that shape the workings of American justice when a man's life is threatened by capital punishment.

When the hearing opened on November 15, Judge Ellis didn't need to hear any more arguments. "My recommendation to the court of Criminal Appeals is that this—that the punishment phase of the trial be relitigated," he said. He then said, "I do not, do not ever want to sign one of those things [death warrant] without knowing that everything that could have been done . . . is done." We were halfway there.

Chapter 52:

Grace from a Garage

"This cannot be what I think it is. It's over."
"Why would a policeman have documents in his garage?"

While we were waiting for that to happen, we received astonishing news. The news got us *all* the way there.

On April 8, 2013, Lynn Hardaway, the district attorney who took over for Hampton, sent an e-mail to Judge Ellis, with a cc: to Casey Kaplan, stating that Officer McDaniel had given her a box of materials he found while "spring cleaning" his garage. She said, correctly, that she wanted to share them with defense counsel.

The next day, the box arrived at Casey's office in Dallas. Casey asked his associate, Megan Whisler, to take a look. As she leafed through the records, she felt pretty sure this was material she had already seen. Then she saw the words "Doby GF landline" scrawled on one of the documents. "Doby" could only refer to Dewayne. "GF" is short for girlfriend, meaning Ericka Dockery.

"This cannot be what I think it is," she was thinking.

She checked the number. She checked it again. She felt like someone who had a winning lottery ticket. She ran out of her office. She walked very fast through the reception area and went up one floor to Casey's office. He was not there. She ran down the hallway to find him, and when she did, she held out the piece of paper.

"It's over," she said.

Megan held the phone record that the police and prosecutors said they didn't have. It was a record of calls made from Ericka Dockery's landline. It showed that there was a call at 10:08 a.m. on April 3, 2003, from Ericka's house to Alma Berry's house. A few minutes later, they called me at my office in Washington.

"Are you sitting down?" Casey asked.

I said yes. He said, "Check your computer."

There it was.

"Yes!!!!!" I screamed. I threw the phone down, danced in place, jumped up and down, smacked my desk as hard as I could, and yelped some more. Some coworkers came by office to see if I was OK.

I was more than OK. We now could prove that Dewayne made the call from Ericka's house. The phone record firmed up the timeline of events and strengthened Dewayne's alibi. He was, as he had been saying for ten years, at Ericka Dockery's house when the murders occurred.

The phone record broke the case wide open.

It also exposed potential wrongdoing. In the box from Officer McDaniel's garage, Casey and Megan also found a subpoena requesting the phone records from Southwestern Bell, signed by none other than DA Rizzo. The subpoena was dated April 24, 2003. This meant that Rizzo had the phone records the whole time before the trial and never turned them over to Dewayne's lawyers.

And then there was this: the subpoena was signed by Rizzo *the day after* Ericka testified in the grand jury. In her testimony, she said that she recognized her number on Alma Berry's caller ID. In seeking the records, Rizzo was trying to determine if she was lying or telling the truth. If he looked at the phone records he obtained, he had good reason to believe she was telling the truth. He charged her with perjury anyway. And he never turned the records over to the defense counsel!

This fact alone would be grounds for a new trial. Rizzo had sworn he didn't have the landline records. He had signed an affidavit in response to our original writ stating, "I did not suppress knowledge of or information about a landline call from Ericka Dockery's apartment to Alma Berry's house." Was that a bold lie or an inadvertent mistake?

I had some opinions about the answer but whatever the case, the failure to turn over the records to Dewayne's trial lawyers was inexcusable and improper and confirmed what I thought all along: that the state was willing to win at any cost. After I finished celebrating the good news, I started feeling angry in a way I had not been angry in a long time. All I could think was, "In a garage? They found the records in a %$#**&' garage?"

When I got home that night, I saw Anna and the girls standing on the front porch, and I started to cry. I told them what had happened, and Anna hugged me and said, very simply, "I never doubted you."

Inquisitive Ella, now nine years old, wanted me to explain it all to her, so I did.

"Why would a policeman have documents in his garage?" she asked. She was smart (and beautiful), like her mother.

Exactly, I said. That night I prayed over and over again in thanks for the turn of events.

We were lucky. Officer McDaniel hadn't pitched that box in the trash after all those years. His house didn't have a flood. Or a fire. His district attorney wife didn't demand that he clean out the garage and pitch the boxes from old cases. If any of those things had happened, DA Rizzo might have gotten away with putting an innocent man to death. And I couldn't take too much solace in our good fortune because I knew Rizzo's conduct was not all that unusual. As Judge Alex Kozinski would write later that year, "There is an epidemic of *Brady* violations about the land."

Our *Brady* violation took place in a garage. Dewayne was just one more victim of that epidemic.

Chapter 53:

The Inadequate Counsel

I was also upset with Loretta Muldrow. If the district attorney was able to sub-poena the records, then defense counsel could have done so, too, or pressed Rizzo really hard for them. If Muldrow had sought out the records before Dewayne's trial and presented them at trial, the jury might have made a different judgment about whether Dewayne participated in the murders. Ericka Dockery might not have felt compelled to change her testimony. Muldrow was aware of the issue. Early on in the case, Bethany had asked her about the phone records. Muldrow replied via email, "Southwestern Bell's landlines to landlines non-toll calls are not obtainable." Well, DA Rizzo got them.

To her credit, when Muldrow was informed that she had not been given the court records, she went to the district attorney's officer and, as Casey told me, "went ballistic." She shouted that Lynn Hardaway should "run, not walk, to the First Assistant DA and elected DA" to get a new trial for Dewayne. Along the way she dropped multiple "f-bombs" and promised to go to the media if Hardaway didn't do the right thing. She also agreed to sign an affidavit for us. In her defense, she could say that she fought the DA in Dewayne's case with one hand tied behind her back because she didn't have all the evidence Dewayne was entitled to.

All of it was a reminder of how close Dewayne came to death.

Chapter 54:

Elected Judges Dither

"Mr. Brown, I'm meaning what I say. We will give you the trial that you deserve."
"Do right and answer God's call."

Not long after that we found out that Jesse Coleman (a.k.a. "Smooth"), the author of the "E.W. letter" that initially sent us on the path to trying to figure out who was the real perpetrator, had been murdered. I said a prayer for Smooth that night, and thanked him for having a conscience and writing to Dewayne.

On May 17, 2013, Casey was scheduled to talk with the District Attorney's Office about the phone records. I knew I wouldn't be able to work, so I took the day off. I delivered the kids to school and camped out at the local public library near my house. At 2:11 p.m., Casey emailed me: "Done deal." The District Attorney himself, Mike Anderson, agreed to a new trial because of the *Brady* violation.

I jumped up out of my chair, threw my hands in the air, and didn't dare say a word to interrupt the silence of the library. So I ran outside and let out another scream, joyful, huge, and soul-lifting. I danced in front of the library and then fell to the ground.

Casey and Megan called to say the DA agreed to a new trial because of the *Brady* violation. Dewayne's case would be assigned to a new prosecutor once Judge Ellis agreed to it at a hearing on May 28 and once the Court of Criminal Appeals agreed with it as well. I hung up, jumped up and down a few times, and danced some more. I ran up to a tree and punched it happily like a boxer, landing many combinations.

I spoke with Anna and she sobbed, and so did I. I called Chris Tate. "How's it feel to bring someone back from the dead?" he asked. I hung up and danced some more.

I planned to fly to Houston on May 27, 2013, Memorial Day, at 9:30 p.m. after a full three-day weekend with the family. We went to the neighborhood pool by our house, had a barbeque, and also went to a campout that night at a pool that we used to belong to. The campout was straight-up Americana—burgers, dogs, corn on the cob, beans in a bowl, s'mores in an open-pit fire, and glow sticks for the kids to run around with. After the kids went to bed in the tents, the dads sat around, drank beer, and talked about nothing important. It was simple perfection. I slept in a tent with Audrey, my sweet six-year-old, who was born when I started working on Dewayne's case. I got up in the middle of the night to go to the bathroom, and surveyed the calm peace as I looked around the sea of tents at the tree-lined park. I thought of Dewayne and the six-by-ten-foot cell. I got really mad, but then instantly peaceful based on what I was about to go do and how close we were.

Two days later, I met Casey on the fourteenth floor of the Criminal Justice Building in Houston, where Judge Ellis's courtroom is located. I gave him a man hug, and said, "Can you frickin' believe this?" Megan was with him. She was perhaps the most important person on the case, because she was the one who found the missing phone record. I joked with her that she should just quit the law right now, because it would never ever get any better than this.

We went into the courtroom, and the Sheriff said Dewayne was ready to be brought in. In the eight years I had known him, we had never touched, only put our hands together separated by a thick shield of glass. The Sheriff put in the key, opened the door, and when Dewayne came out, we were less than a couple feet away. He extended his hand to me, and I looked at the Sheriff for a moment to see if I would be allowed to touch him. I thought about asking, and decided, nah. I didn't need permission. I grabbed Dewayne's hand, pulled him close to me, and gave him the strongest man hug I have ever given. I was crying, I put my hand on the back of his head, put my forehead to his, and said, "I told you we wouldn't give up. I told you."

Then we settled down for the hearing.

First, Casey introduced a statement of facts about the phone records and made the case for a new trial. In her turn, Hardaway agreed. She said that the failure to turn over the phone records was inadvertent. In the "interest of justice," she said Dewayne should get a new trial.

Judge Ellis said he would sign the statement of facts. He then addressed the appellate court directly and said:

"To the guys and gals of the Court of Criminal Appeals, I am signing this because I agree with it. I don't want there to be any doubt in your mind that this—I believe that the circumstances in which we find ourselves at this time merit a new trial in Mr. Brown's case, and I hope that you will follow the findings that I'm signing today, and as soon as practical afford us the opportunity to re-try the case. . . . So, please hurry. Okay?

I couldn't believe what I was hearing.

Judge Ellis then addressed Dewayne directly: "Mr. Brown, I'm meaning what I say. As soon as we can, with the cooperation of the Court of Criminal Appeals, we will give you the trial that you deserve."

The hearing took less than five minutes. Six years after I started working on the case, Dewayne had a new trial and a real shot at freedom.

The Sheriff led Dewayne out of the courtroom and we departed, still in disbelief. We left the courthouse, piled into Casey's car, and went to a Mexican restaurant, where we ordered drinks. When they came, Casey said simply, "To Dewayne." This was not an over-the-top celebration, more a moment of happy reflection.

Around the table, we speculated about what was going to happen next. Casey wondered whether the state would try to save face with the families of the victims and re-try the case, even though they knew they would lose. We talked about the possibility that the state would offer to let Dewayne plead guilty in return for a time-served sentence, to which we all said we would never agree. Maybe the state would offer an "Alford plea," where Dewayne would not plea to anything, but acknowledge that the state had evidence that implicated him, all so he could get time served and be released. Even that didn't suit us. We all focused on the implications of what had just happened, processing it in our own ways.

Before I returned to Washington, I went back to the jail to see Dewayne one more time. We met in the attorney conference room with that familiar pane of thick glass between us.

"How you doing, man?" I asked.

"Real good, man, real good," he said from the other side.

I asked if he understood what had just happened. He said not really. So I explained it as best I could without sounding too legal or complicated. I told him about the documents in the garage, and he said, "What were they doing in the garage?"

"Exactly," I said again.

I asked who had come to see him. He had a few visitors, but not Kiearra. He was concerned that she was getting older and getting into the same things that other growing girls were getting into. His main goal if he got out, he said, was to learn how to read. Without that, he said, he would have a hard time finding a job. I was stunned to hear him say this, and how earnestly he said it.

We talked about music for a while. I told him I loved hip-hop, and my favorite groups were Public Enemy, the Beastie Boys, Eric B. & Rakim, and Gang Starr. I also told him my deepest musical secret that only Anna and my buddy Jimmy from Jersey knew—that my favorite song of all time was "Easy Lover" by Phil Collins and Philip Bailey. He laughed at me. I asked him which musicians he liked, and he told me John Legend, Anthony Hamilton, and 50 Cent. I told him that I loved 50 as well, and asked him if he ever heard "Hate it or Love it," the song that 50 did with The Game. He knew the song and liked it. I told him it was his theme song, and I sang the hook: "Hate it or love it the underdog's on top." He laughed at my attempt to sing.

We talked for about two hours, one of the longest visits we ever had, laughing and joking like old friends, which, in fact, we were. We had known each other for six years. My love for him was just as full that day as the first day I met him, an agape-type love. I loved him selflessly and unconditionally. I felt that one of the reasons I was put on the earth was to get him out of the place he was. I would accept no other result, and it actually began to feel like that result was possible and attainable. I put my hand up to his, and said, "Remember my promise, my man."

And then nothing happened. For months. The Criminal Court of Appeals, or CCA, simply wouldn't rule on whether Dewayne should get a new trial. Everybody had agreed there should be a new trial: the prosecutor, the defense counsel, and the judge. Judge Ellis had even asked them to "hurry up." All the CCA had to do was ratify the agreement.

The CCA announced its decisions every Wednesday. At first I hoped each week that I would soon hear the good news. Summer became fall, and fall became winter. I stopped getting excited about going to work on Wednesdays and just woke up mad. Casey would text me to say, "Another crappy Wednesday," and I usually responded with harsher language. What was the holdup? There was speculation that the judges did not want to issue a positive decision for Dewayne, a "cop killer," in an election year because their opponents would use it against them politically.

As 2013 turned to 2014, we decided to go to the media to see if we could prod the court to act. Casey knew Pam Colloff, a writer for the *Texas Monthly*, who had covered Anthony Graves's case and other exoneration stories. She couldn't take on any new stories, but she referred us to Lisa Falkenberg, a columnist with the *Houston Chronicle*.

When Lisa reviewed some of the documents in the court file, she got very interested and wanted to know more. I could tell that Lisa was careful and thoughtful and smart, but I was still nervous talking to a reporter about a case in which I had so much invested. In time, I came to trust her.

Lisa did not disappoint. Her first story came out on May 13, 2014, almost one year after Judge Ellis's order for a new trial. "Wheels of Justice Grind Slowly on Death Row," said the headline. Lisa presented the history of the case in a straightforward way that questioned why the Criminal Court of Appeals was waiting. She even quoted Judge Ellis. Asked why it was taking so long for the CCA to rule, he said, "I wish I knew." He added, "They move in mysterious ways in Austin."

"Even those whom fate has dealt the cruelest hand are entitled to a fair trial," Lisa wrote in conclusion. "How long is a man who very well could be innocent supposed to sit still and silent on death row while the ladies and gentlemen in black robes take their sweet time dallying over his fate?"

I was very happy with the article, and relieved when the response to it was generally positive. But it was probably naïve to think that one article would get the judges to say, "Oh, sure, here's the new trial." As we crept towards another summer, I wondered when it would ever end. For a few days I was deep in depression, staying up late, watching stupid TV shows, and cursing the judges of the CCA.

It became incredibly clear what the Court of Criminal Appeals was doing. Republican judges were the majority on the Court, and they wanted to keep that status, so they were delaying any ruling on Dewayne's case until after the election in November. You could just picture some campaign manager sitting in a room, saying, "You can't give that guy a new trial now, he was convicted of shooting a police officer. Your opponents will be all over that!" And then you could picture the Republican judges nodding their heads in agreement. It was despicable, and it made me hate Texas even more, if that was possible. It also made me hate a system where judges of any court are elected. Dewayne's rights and due process were simply secondary to political expediency and results, and that just pissed me off. I was depressed and in a very bad place.

I corresponded with Dewayne's pen pal, Magdalena from Switzerland. She was a constant, strong supporter of Dewayne. She sent many encouraging letters and told me that on his birthday she sent him a picture of a lemon cake and all of her friends blowing out the candles. She made me laugh in an e-mail when she wrote that she hoped Dewayne was staying positive. "In Switzerland we say that if you stand in shit up to your chin, you should not hang your head." It was getting hard to hold my head up.

Then my pastor, Jason Micheli, asked me if I would be a guest sermon speaker on Father's Day weekend. He knew Dewayne's story and he had read Lisa's article. Instead of giving a traditional sermon, he wanted to have a conversation with me about the case. His theme in the conversation was to "do right" and to answer God's call when He called, whether it was for a case like Dewayne or for any other event or purpose in someone's life.

I am still humbled by Jason's interest in the case and his insistence that I did God's work in helping Dewayne. I never analyzed the case that way, but after the sermons we did together, I can look back and believe that there was some divine intervention that put Dewayne and I together. Jason put a video of the sermon on his blog (tamedcynic.org) and continued to write thoughtful blog posts about the religious implications of Dewayne's case. He engaged a lot of people in the case and the cause. His timely support was just what I needed to get me out of my depression and back in the right frame of mind and center myself. I loved Jason for that.

I heard from Lisa Falkenberg again. She said she had been doing more reporting and planned to publish a series of stories on the grand jury in Dewayne's case, particularly on how Ericka Dockery was treated. Over the course of two weeks in mid-July 2014, Lisa published four columns that changed the course of Dewayne's case and may have far-reaching implications for the Texas criminal justice system and the way in which grand jurors are selected in the state.

The first was titled "A Disturbing Glimpse into the Texas Grand Jury System," followed by "Mom of 3 Pressured into Changing Story, but Jailed Anyway." In the first story, she describes the "pick-a-pal" or "key-man" grand jury system that prevails in some parts of Texas in which an elected judge picks a grand jury commissioner who then hand-picks grand jurors. In the second story, she recounted how Ericka Dockery had been pressured into changing her story so as to implicate Dewayne in the ACE Cash Express incident. That was a story I knew well. But her final column was a complete surprise to me.

The headline was "Cop Was Foreman of Grand Jury in Cop-Killing," and the story was shocking. The foreman of the grand jury that investigated the ACE Cash Express robbery-murders was a police officer. I remembered being bothered that the foreman had once called Rizzo "Dan" during the grand jury proceedings, and now I knew why.

Lisa identified the man as James Koteras, an active duty Houston Police Department officer. It was completely inappropriate for him to have held that position in a case involving the murder of a fellow officer, and everybody knew it. The current chief of the Houston Police Department, Charles McClelland, told Lisa he would have recused himself from the case. Koteras's participation in the grand jury was "terrible," said Judge Susan Collins, who oversaw the Harris County grand jury system. "That shouldn't have happened. I hope that was an aberration. No, grand jurors don't work for the state."

The disintegration of the case against Dewayne was all but complete.

Chapter 55:

Exoneration

"Never give up."

The election came and went. The Republicans kept their majority on the court. And, of course, the day after the election, the court issued a "per curiam," which means in short, opinion. It was five paragraphs, less than one page. The court held that "the State withheld evidence that was both favorable and material to appellant's case in violation of *Brady*." Therefore, the Court "vacate[d] applicant's conviction and sentence, and remand the case to the trial court for a new trial or other proceeding consistent with this opinion." This size opinion could have been written in a few days after the Court got the case, but it took much longer.

The Court waited *seventeen months* to make this decision. Five hundred and ten days. Judge Ellis told them to hurry, and they waited almost two years for political reasons. Think of everything you have done in your life in the last five hundred days. Dewayne sat in his cell for that long so the court could stay in Republican control. If this doesn't make you mad—well, in my mind, nothing will.

My whole body shook when I read the order. I fell to my knees. Years of stress flowed out of me and joy flowed back in. It finally happened. His conviction was overturned. He was no longer a convicted murderer. He was entitled to the presumption of innocence. I talked with Chris, Bethany, Casey, and Megan. I emailed Dave Case. I emailed Anna, and she said, "I always believed this day would come. So incredibly proud of your dedication! Love you!"

I left work to do the ballet carpool, and when I dropped off all the girls, I went to Taco Bell, my favorite, to grab some celebratory tacos to take home. It was where Anna took me the day I passed the bar. As we ate, I told the kids, "Never give up." Anna and I cried many times during the night.

The next day I went to an NACDL conference about white-collar criminal defense, and the guest speaker was Judge Kozinski. After he spoke, I went up to talk with him and told him about the case and the *Brady* issue. He congratulated me, and I took a picture with him. That evening I spoke at a law school alumni function and was choked up during the speech. Some eager students came up to me after the speech, and I told them the whole story.

The following day, I could not function. My emotions were stirring, and I wanted so badly to fly to Texas to see Dewayne. I took part of the day off and just sat and thought about the case. I went to Jersey Mike's for a sub and saw a police officer, and I thought about Officer Clark's family and how they must be feeling. I prayed for them. Officer Clark's death was a tragedy and should not have happened. I hoped that day they were able to understand that killing Dewayne would have also been a tragedy.

I went home that night and had a lightsaber fight with Andrew on the front lawn. We ended up on the ground with him over me. He jumped into my arms and said, "I am a Jedi like you, Daddy." I smiled. That weekend we did our monthly homeless food service in D.C. The service was pure and good and just what I needed, and I thought about how our collective service to Dewayne was one step closer to freedom.

Ironically, I wound up happy that the appellate court had taken its sweet time, because they gave Lisa Falkenberg time to expose the whole sorry story to the people of Houston and the rest of the world. Her reporting virtually destroyed the prosecution's prospects for winning a conviction at any new trial. She won a Pulitzer for her work, and to her credit, she said that the award did not mean as much as Dewayne's exoneration.

The District Attorney's Office would have to seek a new indictment, but with what evidence? They no longer had the testimony of Erika Dockery, Sharonda Simon, or the Hubbard sisters. And they had the phone record to deal with. They had Shon's testimony but, according to Texas law, accomplice testimony alone could not be the basis of a conviction. In the end, the prosecutors literally had no case.

Another significant part of Lisa's reporting was about to change Texas law. The issue of the "pick-a-pal" grand jury was being heavily debated in the media, with an editorial from the *Houston Chronicle* insisting that "potential jurors should be picked from a random pool taken from public records."

Harris County Judges were calling for the law to be changed. In-depth articles were written about how cozy and subject to cronyism the "pick-a-pal" system was. One article detailed the grand jury service of Patricia Pollard, who was photographed in a Houston Police Department helicopter because she was a grand jury foreperson. The article was called "Patricia Pollard: An example of a system gone wrong." She was supposed to be a neutral, fair arbiter of the evidence presented before her. Instead she was grand jury foreperson on five grand juries and assistant foreman on another, and she was taking ride alongs in helicopters and being chummy with cops and DAs. There was no way she would do anything other than indict Dewayne for allegedly murdering a police officer. I am sure she saw it as her sworn duty to make sure of the indictment. The whole system stunk, and I was glad that not only were we going to get justice for Dewayne, but that the process would be more fair for criminal defendants in the future. No more helicopters and rides, and no more Patricia Pollard. Just fairness.

The bill abolishing the "pick-a-pal" system passed the Texas House and Senate and was signed by Governor Abbott on June 19, 2015, with an effective date of September 1, 2015. Future criminal defendants will not be judged by a stacked deck of cronies; they will have a fair and honest process. Now, no states in the country use this procedure. None. And that's the way it should be.

Interestingly, even amidst all these reports, I didn't see any position taken by Devon Anderson, the District Attorney. She was appointed to take the position held by her husband, Mike Anderson, after he died of cancer. Mike Anderson had agreed to the new trial. Now his widow and successor was up for election in November, and she gave many speeches. Lisa tracked her down and pestered her to state her position on the "pick-a-pal" system. "If I was on the bench today, I would not use the 'key man' system," she said. "I would use the random jury pool."

She then commented on Dewayne's case and the grand jury treatment of Ericka.

"I thought it was shocking," she said. "It would have been interesting to see the witness's demeanor. That's the only thing about transcripts, is that they're flat. If she had a real 'screw you' attitude, that may have accounted for some of it, but it was disturbing. I was troubled."

Anderson said she was confident that current practices in her office would prevent another case like Dewayne's from happening again, saying that prosecutors now check grand juror occupations to make sure no grand jurors who are current or former police officers hear officer-involved shooting cases. Anderson's comments gave some insight into what she thought about the case. I hoped she would dismiss this case rather than have a new trial. I hoped she would do the right thing.

Chapter 56:

A Prayer for Dewayne

In March, I went to New Orleans for the ABA White-Collar Conference. This was an annual conference where defense lawyers from across the country got together for seminars, cocktail parties, and dinners. It was also my first time in New Orleans, which was exciting. It made me feel even more connected to Dewayne, since he loved Louisiana so much. I bought a bag of Zapp's Spicy Cajun Crawtators in his honor and walked down Bourbon Street with the scantily-clad strippers and the drunks drinking hurricanes. I ducked into Musical Legends Park and listened to some mellow jazz played by a trio. They played "Summer Wind" by Frank Sinatra, and it made me think of my Jersey roots and my Uncle Patrick, who introduced me to the song. The bandleader took a request from a tourist from Finland and played "Fly Me to the Moon," so it was back-to-back Sinatra. Perfect for a Jersey boy like me. I ate the chips and a beignet and looked up to the strands of white lights at the outdoor bar. Then I looked up to the sky and took a deep breath.

When I went home, I was invited by Catholic University to give a speech on pro bono service. I talked about Dewayne's case and broke down in tears when I told them that working on Dewayne's case was why I became a lawyer. Some of the students who came to the speech were crying. It was so great to be back at the school, and I thought about how I would love to teach there one day.

After the speech, I went to the shrine on campus and attended a mass in the crypt church. Afterwards, I went upstairs to the shrine. I was the only one there. I walked slowly down the same aisle I walked down seventeen years prior for my law school graduation. I could hear every footstep and feel every breath. I sat in the front pew and stared at the murals. I stared right into a mural of Jesus and got lost in my mind for a few minutes. I said a prayer for Dewayne, Officer Clark, Alfredia Jones, and their families. I then prayed for the district attorney to do the right thing. I closed by giving thanks for the blessing of working on the case. I sat for a few more minutes, stood up and lit a candle, and drove home. It was time.

Chapter 57:

Freedom

"I went in an innocent man and I came out an innocent man."

On New Year's Eve 2014, my family sat and watched the ball drop in Times Square in New York, and Anna came up with an idea—everyone was to write something down on a piece of paper that they wanted to happen in 2015, and we would read them on New Year's Eve the following year. I wrote, simply: "Freedom!"

Almost simultaneously as I wrote that on a piece of paper in my living room, Dewayne was being transported out of death row and brought to Harris County to see whether there would be a retrial. Dewayne later told me that as he left, the inmates on the row cheered for him. One of them told him to send some money for his commissary account. I hoped he would never go back to Polunsky ever again, except to visit his former row mates.

Dewayne was appointed a new defense lawyer, Katherine Scardino, for the retrial. Katherine is well known in the defense bar in Houston. She was Anthony Graves's attorney when he was released. Her investigator called her a "piranha," and that was exactly what we needed. Dewayne was in good hands.

Then it happened. I was driving when I got a text from Lisa on June 8, 2015. There was going to be a DA press conference at 3:00. She didn't know what it was for, but she thought it might be related to Dewayne.

I called Katherine. She had not heard about it and sent an associate to go check it out. A few minutes later, I called Katherine and she conferenced in her associate. Her assistant held the phone up, and I could hear what District Attorney Devon Anderson said. There would be no retrial. The charges were dismissed.

I pulled over and screamed and yelled so loud I thought I was going to break the car window. I jumped up and down in the driver's seat and was spastically throwing myself against the car. I was having an out-of-body experience like I had never had before. I continued to yelp and scream and then cried uncontrollably. I felt like I was going to puke, and almost did.

Katherine said she would call me back when she got more information. She called back a few minutes later and said that he would be released later that day.

"I went in an innocent man and I came out an innocent man," Dewayne told reporters when he emerged. "I'm pretty sure there's many more like me."

He said he had no bitterness. He said that "they [the state] did what they felt was right. Even though it was wrong. I can't blame them for that." He then said, "Nowadays, you can't trust everybody. But you can always love everybody." He left death row speaking words of love, rather than words of hate.

Chapter 58:

Oysters and a Road Trip

"Hate it or Love it, the Underdog's on Top."

There was no way for me to get to Texas that night, so I decided to leave first thing the next morning. Chris and Bethany were also going to fly there. After I heard from Katherine, I went to pick up Audrey from school. She was in second grade and was a precious little girl, inside and out. I saw her from across the baseball field that was next to the school. We started running towards each other like in the movies, and we fell to the ground. I was crying and I told her about Dewayne. She started to cry, too. We got up and she said, "Daddy that's so cool, but you know what? I got my yearbook today!" We sat in the car and read the yearbook together in between my tears. Anna came home, and we hugged for what felt like an hour. We melted into each other and I could feel the joy fill both of us. She was my rock; it meant everything to me. Andrew jumped in, hugged me, and gave me a small toy lightsaber, saying I could keep it for my trip to Texas to give to Dewayne.

That evening I had my annual suburban dad basketball tournament. We play every Monday night; I love my hoop dads. We played best of three games, with two games that night and one the following week. I had T-shirts made to psych out the other team. We were the "Team Red Bull Killers," because the other captain and one of my good friends, Scott Meares, was a big dude with red hair whom we all affectionately called the Red Bull. We won the first game with a jumper from me at the top of the key off a screen. During the second game, I saw the texts of pictures of Dewayne outside the jail during a press conference. He was out. He was free. He said his lawyers were his "angels from heaven." I took a knee, started to cry, and my buddies congratulated me. It was awesome.

When I got home from the hoops game, I called Dewayne. He said, "Wow, I can't believe it." He said freedom "felt funny, but a good kinda funny." I told him he would have to get used to it, and he said he thought he could. He said he went with pure emotion at the press conference, and he spoke from his heart. I told him I was proud of him, and I couldn't wait to see him the next morning. I told him not to leave Houston, and he laughed. "For you, I will wait. Lookin' forward to it, man."

I boarded a 5:40 a.m. flight from D.C. to Charlotte with a connection to Houston. I felt emotions like I had never felt before. I broke out into tears and laughter at various times. I took a deep breath and put on my old friend David Gray on the iPod. Then I played "Fight the Power" and Dewayne's theme song, "Hate it or Love it" by 50 Cent, for old time's sake. I smiled and said, "Goddamn right, the underdog is on top." I fell asleep.

On my way to Texas, I spoke with Kathryn Kase from Texas Defender Services, who sent us the case initially. She also said what we did was a mitzvah, and in Judaism, when you save one life, you save the entire world. I thanked Kathryn for giving me the case of my career and my life.

I met Bethany at the gate in Houston. I had not seen her in years. We hugged and said, "Can you believe it?" We coordinated with Chris and Suzette on the way into Houston, and we all got to the place where Dewayne was at the same time. He was staying with Connie's daughter, who lived in a newer version of the VA near the airport.

Then I saw him. I saw Dewayne. I ran up to him and hugged him and he lifted me up. I hugged him so tight, I didn't want to let him go. I held his head and said, "I told you, man, I told you this day would come." He laughed and smiled and hugged me again. I could not stop touching him. "Is it really you?" I asked.

Then I saw Kiearra and had the same emotion. I hugged her and cried and told her that I was so happy her Daddy was back. She said, "Thank you," and buried her head into my chest. I told her I loved her.

We got to Katherine's office and Lisa was waiting for us. She talked to Dewayne for a few minutes about how it felt to get out and what he did when he got out. He described the first thing he ate—a Whataburger chicken sandwich with chicken tenders on Texas Toast. His sister made enchiladas. He watched two movies, *Fast and Furious 6* and *The Lone Ranger*. He had not slept since he got out, and was not tired. He spoke with Lisa with a composure and a peace that was amazing to see. He was sweet, funny, and self-deprecating. While he was in prison, some folks sent him "Cat in the Hat" books. He said he wanted to learn to read.

We went into Katherine's office for a television interview. We were all worried the moment would be too much for him. I made some scathing comments about how messed up the Texas justice system was, but they did not air those parts. Dewayne did a great job with the questions; he was poised and comfortable. We all agreed that this was the last media statement he was going to make for a while. It was time for him to go home.

Before we left, we went to go get the food he was craving—raw oysters. We went to Goode Company Seafood, close to Katherine's office, and he ate twelve oysters. The horseradish made him cry, and he laughed about that. For dessert, he had a huge piece of pecan pie with ice cream on it. It was simply perfect. I sat next to Kiearra and laughed with her and hugged her.

Before we left, I got a text that Megan was coming from Dallas to see Dewayne. She came to the restaurant and hugged him. I asked her if she wanted to tag along for a road trip to take Dewayne home, and she agreed right away. We were too many for my car, so we rented a minivan for a good old-fashioned road trip.

Dewayne went to the hospital to see a sick aunt, and an hour or so later we were all at the apartment where we first saw him. We packed his things. All he had to his name was a small brown lunch bag from the jail with his name on it, a few shirts that he got the night before from Walmart, two pairs of jeans, and a small plastic bag with socks and underwear.

The road trip was perfect, too. We ate junk food at gas stations. We did a midnight McDonald's run, and played a whole lot of music. Chris had a playlist of the hundred best hip-hop songs, and we listened to everybody from Eric B. & Rakim to Nas to Mobb Deep to Tupac. My favorite moment came when we played "Hate it or Love it" for Dewayne. We all sang along, and it was awesome.

Chapter 59:

"Live your life. Live it."

"I love you."
"I love you, too, man."

We finally dropped Dewayne off at a family member's house many miles away from Houston. We didn't stay long because we had a long car ride home. Before we left, I gave him some money we had all pooled together and told him we would always be there for him.

I held his head in my hands. "Live your life," I said. "Live it." He nodded. I then paused and said, "I love you."

"I love you, too, man." He got into a car with his cousins and went to go see his ninety-two-year-old grandmother for the first time in over a decade. He couldn't wait to hug her.

We drove back to Houston. I slept most of the way and woke up in the Houston airport parking garage. It was time to go home. On the plane home, I started reading some of the newspaper coverage from the case, including an editorial in the *Chronicle* that was titled, simply, "An innocent man." I did the Jumble, and the first two words were "divine" and "effort." Score another one for divine intervention. When I got back home, we gathered up the kids from their activities and went to dinner to celebrate at—where else?—Taco Bell.

Chapter 60:

What Can Be Done?

"Here in Texas, we tell people that if you commit really bad crimes, we're going to put you to death."

When I tell Dewayne's story to people, many are shocked—the documents in a garage, a friendly cop on the grand jury—and they ask, "How do you stop this from happening again?" My answer is always, "Abolish the death penalty." When they laugh and say that will never happen, I say that that is the only way to prevent the execution of innocent people. And I don't agree with them when they say it will never happen, because I think it will.

Troy Davis said it best in a letter to supporters before he died: "The fight to end the death penalty is not won or lost through me but through our strength to move forward and save every innocent person in captivity across the globe. We need to dismantle this unjust system city by city, state by state, and country by country."

I accept that in states like Texas, Oklahoma, Florida, and even my home state of Virginia, most people are in favor of capital punishment. Executions will likely continue, albeit in lower numbers. But I doubt very much that even the most fervent supporters of the death penalty are comfortable with the possibility that an innocent person might be put to death. So, leaving aside the arguments over abolition, there are actions that we can take right now to reduce the chances that people will be put to death for crimes they did not commit.

Texas actually took two very large steps towards those goals in 2013 with the Michael Morton Act. The law is named after a man who was convicted of a murder by a district attorney in Williamson County, Ken Anderson, who deliberately hid exculpatory evidence during Morton's trial. The judge assigned to review the case said, "This Court cannot think of a more intentionally harmful act than a prosecutor's conscious choice to hide mitigating evidence so as to create an uneven playing field for a defendant facing a murder charge and a life sentence." Anderson was convicted, sentenced to ten days in jail, and ordered to surrender his law license. Morton was freed.

The Michael Morton Act broadens the disclosure obligations of Texas prosecutors, requiring them to give defense counsel all police reports and witness statements in a case, regardless of whether the evidence is material to guilt or punishment. This requirement goes beyond even the federal *Brady* obligations. But an unscrupulous prosecutor can still shirk these obligations and most likely get away with it.

The second new law is even more significant, requiring the Department of Public Safety to perform DNA testing "on all biological evidence" collected during an investigation and requiring the state to pay for the testing. This law became effective on September 1, 2013. "This modest but vitally important reform will help reduce the possibility that the ultimate mistake is made with someone receiving the ultimate penalty," said former State Senator Rodney Ellis, who sponsored the law. This measure could dramatically reduce the number of wrongful convictions in capital punishment cases.

Yet such new measures, while welcome, are no panacea. The new laws would not have helped Dewayne. The mandatory disclosure law would not have forced release of the phone record. The DNA testing law would not have helped, because there was no significant DNA evidence in his.

Dewayne was convicted by accomplice testimony and by witnesses who said they saw what they saw because they were pressured to say so. To mitigate the danger of such cases, I recommend that if we have to have the death penalty, there should be a law that bars prosecutors from seeking it unless they possess an element of biological, scientific, or what I will call "electronic evidence," such as video surveillance imagery. Eyewitness testimony is simply too unreliable and contributes to a significant number of erroneous convictions. As the National Registry of Exonerations (www.exonerationregistry.org) reported in 2014, "perjury from witnesses was found to be the biggest problem for those wrongfully convicted of murder."

The reform I propose is not novel. Maryland had such a law until it repealed the death penalty altogether in 2013. It required the state provide evidence of one of the following in death penalty cases: (1) biological evidence or DNA evidence that links the defendant to the act of murder; (2) a videotaped, voluntary interrogation and confession of the defendant to the murder; or (3) a video recording that conclusively links the defendant to the murder. The law also stated that a defendant could not be sentenced to death, only life without parole, "if the state relies solely on evidence provided by eyewitnesses." If death penalty states like Texas, Oklahoma, Florida, and Virginia adopted such a law, we all could sleep a little better at night. Dewayne could not have been sentenced to death under that law.

In addition, any state that executes people needs to have an Innocence Commission empowered to review cases of alleged innocence. One model, the North Carolina Innocence Inquiry Commission, has screened hundreds of cases and can recommend judicial review to a three-judge panel. That panel has the ability to overturn a conviction, which it has done nine times.

We need to bolster the death penalty bar. That means increased and stable funding for attorneys who defend indigent people accused of capital crimes. I am on a list of court-approved counsel in federal court in Maryland and Washington D.C. who can take court-appointed criminal cases. I take every referral I get very seriously. But after Dewayne's case, it is clear to me that the system of providing competent counsel to indigent defendants is broken. I am not alone in this feeling. At a Justice Department event commemorating the fiftieth anniversary of *Gideon*, Attorney General Eric Holder said, "America's indigent defense system exists in a state of crisis." It is time, he declared, "to reclaim Gideon's petition— and resolve to confront the obstacles facing indigent defense providers."

We need to have a clear compensation and social service system for exonerees so they can rebuild their lives. Glenn Ford was denied compensation by Louisiana because the state alleged that he knew who committed the crime and may have been more involved than the facts indicated. He was given a twenty-dollar gift card from the state, and it lasted him one meal. He died penniless, and that was simply wrong; it exacerbated his injustice.

In Texas, the state does provide a generous compensation structure for exonerees, but the district attorney has to file an affidavit of "actual innocence," or the court has to base the relief given to a defendant on actual innocence. In this case, even though Devon Anderson did the right thing by dismissing the charges, and Dewayne is actually innocent, for political reasons she will not file such an affidavit. This means that Dewayne may have to wage another legal battle, this time with a contested compensation petition against the state, or potentially a civil rights lawsuit in federal court. States should have fewer legal barriers for exonerees to be compensated for the injustice they suffered. No one should die like Glenn Ford again.

Finally, prosecutors should be investigated, criminally punished, and disbarred in cases where evidence was deliberately withheld. The sanctioning of Ken Anderson in the Michel Morton case was a groundbreaking development in criminal law. The prosecutor in the Anthony Graves case, Charles Sebesta, was disbarred in 2016 for using false testimony and withholding evidence. The possibility that a prosecutor might be referred to the courts for ethical violations and might lose his or her law license would create an incentive not to abuse power.

We certainly needed that in Dewayne's case. I think an investigation should be conducted to see if criminal charges and/or disbarment proceedings are warranted against DA Rizzo. A couple weeks after the reversal, the *Houston Chronicle* ran a story that Houston's largest organization of criminal defense lawyers demanded an investigation of Rizzo for his conduct in the case. Rizzo denied any misconduct, according to the story, Rizzo said prosecutors typically subpoena voluminous amounts of documents, and he did not know the officer had the phone record. He then said the jury in Brown's trial heard the "substance of the alibi" about the phone call. What? The jury heard the "substance of the alibi," and it was fine that the actual phone record was not turned over? It only proved his alibi after all.

I wanted to fly to wherever Rizzo was in his retirement and yell at him. His statement was so telling about how justice is doled out in Houston: "Oh, it's OK he didn't get the record that would have definitively showed he was home. The jurors heard that was his defense, so that was enough." It was paternalism mixed with arrogance. He issued the subpoena the day after Ericka testified in the grand jury about the call from her house, so he was trying to disprove her with the records, and when it came back that it actually supported Dewayne, it was not turned over. If it was not intentional, and it was just sloppy or negligent, then that is unacceptable as well. That day I was glad Rizzo was on a golf course, not a courtroom.

Any action to hold Rizzo accountable would be an important symbolic event and might finally put enough fear in the District Attorney's Office to follow the rules and play fair. That is unlikely to happen. Rizzo has since retired, and I doubt his former colleagues want to revisit his actions. But even if they did, and even if he were convicted, and even if he served ten days in jail like Ken Anderson, it would be a joke compared to the twelve years Dewayne had to serve. We need to be realistic about the limits of reform, but if prosecutors start suffering real consequences, it will send a message to others.

While I was writing this book, Texas "celebrated" its five hundredth execution since the reinstitution of the death penalty in 1976. On June 26, 2013, Kimberly McCarthy, convicted of murdering her elderly neighbor, was put to death. I don't use the word "celebrate" ironically. After Ms. McCarthy, there were thirty-seven more as of the time I am writing, and probably many more by the time you read this.

"Here in Texas, we tell people that if you commit really bad crimes, we're going to put you to death," said Jim Willett, a former warden and current director of the Texas Prison Museum in Huntsville, Texas, after McCarthy's execution. "And we're going to follow through with it." Those are dangerous words to people who care about justice.

I think the arbitrary nature of American death penalty justice is reason enough to dismantle the whole system. Dewayne's case, while it had a happy ending, was a very close call. Too close. Dave Case could have ignored the email from Texas Defender Service seeking a big firm to take on Dewayne's case. K&L Gates could have declined to take the case. I could have turned the case down when Dave asked me to do it. I could have abandoned the case when the financial and professional pressures were too great. Bethany Nikfar and Chris Tate could have said no. Casey Kaplan and Megan Whisler could have decided not to take over the case. Ericka Dockery could have stayed quiet. Officer McDaniel could have thrown the box of evidence in the trash. It should not require all of these contingent circumstances to save an innocent man from execution.

I'm with Supreme Court Justice Harry Blackmun, who famously declared in a legendary seven-thousand-word dissent on a Texas death penalty case in 1994, "From this day forward, I no longer shall tinker with the machinery of death." It's time for all of us to stop tinkering.

More and more Americans feel the same, which is why the death penalty is dying. While supporters of capital punishment are still in the majority, they seem to be losing ground. A 2014 Gallup poll revealed that 63 percent of respondents favor capital punishment, comparable to what other recent polls have found. That level of support, however, is down from a high of 80 percent in 1994. Other polls suggest that a majority (52 percent) prefer a life without parole sentence over the death penalty, a number I believe will increase as more people question the death penalty.

Only nine states carried out death sentences in 2012, and only forty-three death sentences were carried out across the country, the same as 2011, but down from eighty-five in 2010. In 2013, nine states carried out thirty-nine executions. In 2014, only seven carried out thirty-five executions. In 2015, seven states carried out twenty-eight executions, with thirteen in Texas. The numbers, and public support, will continue to fall, until the practice itself falls.

Which brings us back to Antonin Scalia.

Chapter 61:

Scalia Was Wrong

"Most of us intuitively believe that if the right to due process means anything at all, it means you won't be executed for a crime you didn't commit." —Radley Balko

Antonin Scalia was one of the leading intellectual defenders of the death penalty. If he was the best of the pro-death penalty party—and he probably was—their cause is in trouble. As cases like Dewayne's accumulate and expose the inherent flaws in the death penalty system, Scalia responded with a revealing detachment from reality.

In 2006, Scalia wrote a concurring opinion in a death penalty case, stating, with his usual self-assurance, that "one cannot have a system of criminal punishment without accepting the possibility that someone will be punished mistakenly. That is a truism, not a revelation."

Presumably the conclusion that Scalia, the proud Catholic, wanted us to draw is that innocent people will be executed in America, and we should treat this as axiomatic, not something to be unduly concerned about. Even people who favor capital punishment may pause at this blithe formulation. We shouldn't treat the execution of an innocent person as a revelation, but as a "truism"?

Scalia's own arguments, in their obtuse confidence, actually served to illuminate the weakness of his arguments. When Scalia argued before Troy Davis's execution that there was nothing unconstitutional about executing an innocent man, Ian Millhiser, a blogger for *Think Progress*, dryly observed, "One wonders why we even bother to have a Constitution."

The religion of Scaliaism is so infatuated with Scalia's brilliance that it fails as common sense. "Most of us intuitively believe that if the right to due process means anything at all, it means you won't be executed for a crime you didn't commit," wrote *Washington Post* legal blogger Radley Balko in response to Scalia's outburst. "Or to put it another way, any system that not only allows an innocent person to be executed, but also is okay with it after the fact is, by definition, a system unconcerned with due process."

And that is the legal system that Scalia blessed with bombast, a system that he says should be ultimately unconcerned with due process for the unjustly condemned. How un-American! How unconstitutional! One of Scalia's more bombastic statements about the death penalty as necessary and important in this country was in the case of Henry Lee McCollum, who was convicted of the rape and murder of a young girl. Scalia said, "For example, the case of an eleven-year old girl raped by four men and then killed by stuffing her panties down her throat . . . How enviable a quiet death by lethal injection compared with that!" McCollum was exonerated in 2014 by DNA evidence, and pardoned by Governor Pat McCrory. In Scalia's justice system, Henry Lee McCollum would be dead and have died in an "enviable" way, while in actuality, he was innocent of the crime.

No wonder the death penalty is losing credibility and adherents. No wonder fewer and fewer states practice it. No wonder more and more jurisdictions are abandoning it in favor of life without parole. Scalia exposed the threadbare ethics and contorted logic that underpin the death penalty in America.

Scalia sensed that his arguments were failing. In a speech in September 2015, he said he "wouldn't be surprised" if his colleagues on the court abolished the death penalty. He didn't explain his thinking, but I hope he is right. Justice Kennedy said in a recent opinion that "the Eighth Amendment's protection of dignity reflects the Nation we have been, the Nation we are, and the Nation we aspire to be." Perhaps this is a foreshadowing of how he is leaning.

I cringe when I think Scalia might have analyzed Dewayne's case and let him be executed rather than examine the facts of the matter or question his own certitudes. He would have rested easy thinking Dewayne would have had an "enviable" manner of death. I worry that his legacy of rulings may allow other innocent people to die. But in a way, I welcome his arguments because, like the facts of Dewayne's case, they serve to show that the death penalty is unsustainable under the American constitution.

In the fall of 2015, Pope Francis came to Washington, D.C., and spoke to a joint session of Congress. He stressed the need to have a global abolition of the death penalty. Even Newt Gingrich was so moved by the speech that he said our country had to "profoundly rethink" our criminal justice system.

Scalia wasn't at the Pope's speech. I wasn't, either, but I did see the Pope when he was in D.C., at the Papal Mass at Catholic University. One of the intercessions was to pray for the abolition of the death penalty, and I thought of Dewayne and prayed very hard for that. I hope, like my many, many prayers for Dewayne's release all these years, that that prayer will come true as well.

Chapter 62:

"It don't come down to nothing except love in the end."

As if it were fate, Anna and I had tickets to see David Gray in concert at Wolf Trap on June 16, soon after Dewayne was released. Anna and I walked along the bridge that led to the amphitheater, looked behind us, and saw a beautiful sunset. During the concert, I felt like he was serenading me personally. I thanked him for his songs and for giving me the strength to work on Dewayne's case. I sang along and jumped around like a fool. As the concert ended, I looked up to the stars and thought that Dewayne was home, looking at the same stars. I cried and cried as David sang the song Anna and I love, "Please Forgive Me."

As we walked out of the concert, I sang in my head one of his best lines: "You know, it don't come down to nothing except love in the end." Love and justice prevailed. My post-Dewayne-exoneration life had begun.

Acknowledgments

I sometimes can't believe this all happened. I remember going to death row for the first time like it was yesterday. Now I spend time with Dewayne like we are long-lost brothers. I know the years in between were extremely hard and the mission nearly insurmountable, but I don't even think about that anymore. I just think about Dewayne and his new life, and I am instantly peaceful and happy.

There are so many people to thank, from those who worked on the case to those who helped me navigate the first-time author process. I fear I will forget someone—please know it is not on purpose.

To start, I would like to thank all the attorneys, paralegals, and staff who worked on Dewayne's case. I'm the fortunate one who gets to tell the story, but this quest for justice took a selfless, extraordinary effort by many amazing people. The biggest thank you goes to Kathryn Kase and Texas Defender Service, who had the vision to see the injustice in Dewayne's case. Kathryn and her team fights the good fight every day, and I am forever grateful to her for taking the time to review Dewayne's case and get him dedicated counsel. She is a treasure to the legal community and the death penalty bar, and I encourage you to support her and the work of TDS.

To Dave Case of K&L Gates, my former law firm, for answering the call from Kathryn to take on the case and for convincing the firm to take the case pro bono. For everyone from the firm and others who worked on the case—Dave, Casey Kaplan, Bethany Benitez, Chris Tate, Megan Whisler, Jane Nilan, Jill Lansden, Craig Gaver, Rayco Cheney, Lauren Pryor, and many others. Your constant and unwavering dedication to Dewayne and his case was inspiring, and we will always share a very special bond.

I am especially thankful to Casey, who agreed to take the case over from me when I left the firm, and who set in motion the critical events that led to the uncovering of the phone record that secured Dewayne's exoneration. I am also grateful to Casey for his work in getting media attention for the case. I have relied on Casey many times for his sage advice and guidance. Your humility and steady advocacy for Dewayne was beyond words, and I am proud to call you a "Brother in Brown."

Thank you to those in the field who worked on the investigative phase of the case, Suzette Ermler, Richard Reyna, and Texas death row exoneree Anthony Graves. Suzette is like family to Dewayne—her dedication to him and to the truth was truly inspiring. I will always be grateful for her work. I am especially thankful for Anthony's decision to "pay it forward" and help another death row inmate seek justice. I encourage you to check out the Anthony Graves Foundation and support his efforts to help other innocent individuals in prison.

To Katherine Scardino, who agreed to take on Dewayne's case for the retrial that never happened: You are a living legend, having represented the last two Texas death row exonerees. Someone should write a book about you!

To Neal Manne, Shawn Raymond, and Joe Grinstein from Susman Godfrey, who agreed to help continue the fight for Dewayne in seeking compensation for him for his years of wrongful imprisonment: I am honored that you took up the cause. To Rodney Ellis, who supported Dewayne in a press conference on the day we filed his compensation petition, and for your advocacy of those who need it the most.

To the journalists who reported on the case—Lisa Falkenberg, Pam Colloff, Colby Itkowitz, Radley Balko, Craig Melvin, Samantha Wender, and Emily Drew: as a lawyer, we are usually told to be leery of the media, but each of you proved worthy of trust and respect for the dedication to your craft and your desire to dig in and review the facts to present an independent view. Special thanks to Jon Lenzner, who helped me navigate the media issues in the case and provided me with invaluable guidance and support.

To my legal mentors and teachers who inspired me to be passionate advocates for my clients: It all began with Melinda Douglas at the Alexandria Public Defender's Office my first summer of law school. Melinda taught me that in every defendant charged with a crime there is an individual story to uncover, that justice only happened when everyone in the system played fair, and that it was our job to make sure that happened. Then it was Fred Bennett, who taught criminal procedure and a death penalty seminar with a fire and passion that lit up the room. Then it was Robert Bonsib and Bruce Marcus, who trained me as a young lawyer and who remain the finest attorneys I have ever worked with. They are zealous advocates who exemplify the finest traits in our profession. I try to model myself after Bob and Bruce in every case I work on, but I know I fall short of their models.

Then it was Judge Michele D. Hotten, a true legal trailblazer as the first African-American woman judge on the Circuit Court for Prince George's County, Maryland, and who is now on Maryland's highest appellate court. Judge

Hotten taught me the values of hard work, humility, and giving everyone before her a fair judicial process with no exceptions. Everyone should start one's legal career working for Judge Hotten.

Then it was off to New York, where I worked for a true legend of the defense bar—Bob Morvillo at the white-collar criminal defense boutique, Morvillo Abramowitz. Bob was passionate and fought hard for his clients and, despite the tough image he portrayed, he was a humble man who didn't take himself too seriously, which I admired. And now his sons, Greg and Scott, whom I am fortunate to call friends, carry on that honorable tradition. I am also grateful to Barry Bohrer, who mentored me with his unique brand of humor and style. I made lifelong friends from that firm who have all turned out to be the advocates that Bob taught us to be, like Dave Feldman, Rob Radick, Liz Small, Alvin Bragg, Noah Genel, Stephen Juris, Andrew "Pants" St. Laurent, Rebecca Ricigliano, Danny Rashbaum, Ben Fischer, and, of course, "Sweet Johnnie" Chun.

Then it was the Legal Aid Society in Brooklyn, New York: those years solidified my desire to fight for the indigent and marginalized in society. Being a public defender is a true calling, and I am most proud of those years of my career. I learned from hardworking true believers like Andy Eibel and Mark Whalen, and worked with many young attorneys who were all working towards one goal— fighting for the little guys and protecting their rights. I am especially proud to know young attorneys like Titus Mathai, who started as a public defender right out of law school and became a passionate advocate right before my eyes.

My thanks go to Barry Hartman at K&L Gates, who was a mentor to me, who gave me the opportunity to work on many interesting cases, and who helped me during the challenging times in Dewayne's case and in my career.

And thanks to my current firm, LeClair Ryan, who embraced the story and permitted me to take time out of the office to talk about Dewayne's case and keep up the fight to get him compensation. Special thanks go to Erik Gustafson, Buddy Allen, Gary LeClair, David Freinberg, David Warrington, Mike Holm, Tom Coulter, Laurin Mills, Mike Barnsback, Paris Sorrell, Les Machado, Matt Haynes, Sarah Moffett, Jon Gold, Andy Clark, Ann Micka, my former assistant Maiko Davidson, and my current assistant Kimberly Houston, for all of your support on Dewayne's case. You all owe me lunch at Hard Times Café for putting you in the acknowledgments, by the way.

To Judges Paul L. Friedman and Emmett G. Sullivan of the United States District Court for the District of Columbia and Alex Kozinski of the United States Court of Appeals for the Ninth Circuit: thank you for holding the government to their *Brady* obligations and making sure the defendants before them receive a constitutionally fair judicial process. To Judge Roger W. Titus of the United States District Court for the District of Maryland, in front of whom I tried my first federal criminal case: Even though I "came in second" at that trial, Judge Titus gave my client a fair and thorough hearing, showing me what a model federal judge is. And to my friend and recent appointee to the District Court, Amit Mehta, thank you for your support. You are the model of what the next generation of federal judges should be.

To The Catholic University of America, Columbus School of Law: Thanks for giving me my first-rate legal education and for your consistent support of Dewayne's case. From Deans Veryl Miles to Dan Attridge, I am proud of the way the school supported Dewayne's story. Thank you to Katie Crowley, who heard me speak about the case as a student and later organized a presentation for me to bring Dewayne back to school to tell his story with him. Thank you also to the Alumni Council for supporting me and the case.

To those in the fight, from my personal hero, Sister Helen Prejean; to the Catholic Mobilizing Network and Karen Clifton; Virginians for Alternatives to the Death Penalty; Mid-Atlantic Innocence Project; to Kathryn Kase at Texas Defender Service; to my fellow Board members at Texas Defender Service; to Richard and Sam Branson, who use their status and power for good; to Witness to Innocence and the courageous exonerees who tell their stories; to Mike Farrell and Death Penalty Focus; to the local abolitionists on the ground like the amazing, one-of-a-kind dynamo Pat Hartwell, who do what they do every day with one goal in mind—abolishing the death penalty: I believe your work will come to fruition one day. I hope Dewayne's story helps show the world why. And to the men and women on death row and in prisons across the country who are innocent or the victims of injustice: do not stop fighting for your freedom.

To my family and friends who supported me during the many years I worked on the case: You put up with me talking about the case at lunches, parties, and any other chance I could get. Thank you for listening and encouraging me. To my Aunt Patti and Aunt Leona, Uncle Patrick, and my cousins Patrick Henry, Kevin, Stephanie, and Lisa: your support and love meant a lot. To my father, Robert Stolarz, thank you for instilling in me my work ethic, passion, and sense of humor. Thanks to my mother, Dorothy Stolarz, who died before she got a chance to meet Dewayne, but prayed for him on her deathbed. To Kathy Sidorow, I am grateful for your kindness and love to my family and for your support of Dewayne's case. Thanks as well to my sister, Jessica Stolarz, who has persevered despite a learning disability to be a hard-working, loving person.

Special thanks to my friends Ozzy Jimenez and Carlos Lamas, who always believed in me, who sponsored a presentation I did with Dewayne in Washington, D.C., and who organized a once-in-a-lifetime evening at a Washington Wizards game, including a shoot around in the practice gym at the Verizon Center. To see Dewayne go from an enclosed rec yard that was a slab of concrete to chucking three-pointers was one of the greatest moments of my life. And yes, Ozzy, I made the jumper from behind the arc before you did. . . .

And speaking of hoops, to my Monday Night Suburban Dad Hoops guys: you not only put up with me talking about Dewayne's case, you also put up with my constant trash talk and stupid trick shots. It was fitting that on the night Dewayne was released, I played ball with you fine fellas, and I hit the game-winning shot! Thank you Scott (Red Bull), Carl, Greg, Pat, Nick C., Nick B., Matt, Inman, Aris, Andrew, Drew, Chip, Jeff, BK, Norton, both Tonys, Kyle (you played once, but I will put you in because you are like a brother to me), and the guy with the sweetest stroke in all of Northern Virginia, William "Summer Breeze" Fischer. Thanks for being the coolest group of guys I could ever ask for.

To my spiritual mentors, who taught me to love God, serve others, and always do the right thing: from Father Michael Carnevale to Father Kevin Downey to Father John Enzler, I have been blessed with faithful leaders who built and fortified my spiritual foundation. Thank you to Jim Bishop and M. J. Morrow at Catholic Charities for the Archdiocese of Washington for your prayers and support. Thank you to Reverend Dennis Perry and the smartest theologian I know, Reverend Jason Micheli, who taught me more about myself than I like to admit and whom I love like my own brother. Jason, I am proud of the way you kicked cancer's ass and showed courage for not just you, but for all of us. Thank you to the entire Aldersgate community for your love and support, especially Sue Crane, Val Gass, and Terri Phillips.

Thank you to my cultural inspirations. I have never met any of you, but you shaped who I am, how I see the world, and you gave me the strength and courage to keep fighting for Dewayne no matter the odds. To Spike Lee, who showed me how to "Do the Right Thing;" to Chuck D., who taught me to "Fight the Power;" to Guru, who taught me about the "Conspiracy;" to Eminem, who told me to be "Not Afraid" to take a stand; to Rage Against the Machine, who told me to "Take The Power Back;" to 50 Cent, who showed me how the "underdog's on top;" to David Gray, Bono, and Seal, who taught me how to love instead of hate: thanks to all of you. And thank you to a cultural inspiration I recently met, Jackson Browne. You taught me that "the river opens for the righteous." Thank you for your dedication to social justice.

To Ron Goldfarb and Gerrie Sturman at Goldfarb & Associates: Ron believed in me and my story from the moment I met him, and that meant everything to me. Not only is he an amazing agent, he is a mentor and role model for an honorable career and life. Everything he said would happen with this book happened, and I am forever grateful for his belief in me. I am also thankful for his good humor—I am forever his "Jersey Boy" client. Thank you to Gerrie for always encouraging me, and for your perseverance in seeking the right publisher.

To Jeff Morley, who took my initial draft and made it into an amazing manuscript worthy of publication. Jeff taught me a lot about writing and focus and themes. Thank you, Jeff, for making my book a priority. There is no doubt the book would not be as good as it is now without your help.

To my early readers, who read early drafts of the book and gave me feedback and creative ideas: Thank you to Jenny Larkin, Pat Kretzer, Jay Heimbach, Katie Calogero, Scott Inman, Liz Saladini, and my amazing wife, Anna, for encouraging me and believing that this story could be a book that inspired others.

To Skyhorse Publishing, who took on a first-time author and created the work you have in your hands: You are all true professionals. I am thankful for your hard work and dedication to the project. Thank you to Mark Gompertz for his vision, and Chris Evans for his excellent editing work and guidance on all aspects of the publishing process.

To Anna: There are no words I can write here that will express my gratitude and love for you. We started out with nothing but love and available credit in a tiny studio apartment in Alphabet City in New York, and now we have a full life with three little people I love raising with you. Thank you for always believing in me and in Dewayne, especially during the challenging times in the case and my career. You are my Buddy and my strength forever.

To the kiddos, Ella, Audrey, and Andrew: Thank you for all your support of your Daddy when he was in Texas for days on end trying to right one wrong. May you have the courage and strength to do that in your life's work as well. And may you have many, many, many years with "Uncle Dewayne."

Finally, and most importantly, to Dewayne: You are my brother. I love you and always will. Thank you for the privilege of working on your case and for letting me share your story with the world.

Bibliography

Court Documents and Cases:

Trial record, *State of Texas v. Alfred Dewayne Brown*, Cause No. 1035159, 351st District Court, Harris County, Texas.

Application for a Writ of Habeas Corpus, Cause No. 1035159, 351st District Court, Harris County, Texas, October 24, 2007, and supplemental submissions of evidence filed on May 29, 2008, August 8, 2012, October 25, 2012, and April 11, 2013.

Agreed Proposed Findings of Fact, Conclusions of Law and Order, Cause No. 1035159, 351st District Court, Harris County, Texas, May 22, 2013 and May 28, 2013.

Opinion and Order, *Ex Parte Alfred Dewayne Brown*, No. WR-68,876-01, Court of Criminal Appeals of Texas, November 5, 2014. Mandate issued December 1, 2014.

Atkins v. Virginia, 536 U.S. 304 (2002)

Berger v. United States, 295 U.S. 78 (1935)

Brady v. Maryland, 373 U.S. 83 (1963)

Callins v. Collins, 510 U.S. 1141 (1994)

Gideon v. Wainwright, 372 U.S. 335 (1963)

Glossip v. Gross, 135 S.Ct. 2726 (2015)

In re Troy Davis, 130 S.Ct. 1 (2009) (Scalia Dissent)

Kyles v. Whitney, 514 U.S. 419 (1995)

Woodward v. Alabama, 134 S.Ct. 405 (2013)

United States v. Olsen, 737 F.3d 625 (9th Cir. 2013)

Websites:

Amnesty International U.S. Death Penalty Facts

www.amnestyusa.org/our-work/issues/death-penalty/us-death-penalty-facts

Catholic Mobilizing Network to End the Use of the Death Penalty, www.catholicsmobilizing.org

Death Penalty Focus, www.deathpenalty.org

Death Penalty Information Center, www.deathpenaltyinfo.org

Equal Justice Initiative, www.eji.org

Gallup Polls Regarding Death Penalty, www.gallup.com/poll/1606/death-penalty.aspx

Mid-Atlantic Innocence Project, www.exonerate.org

Sister Helen Prejean, Ministry Against the Death Penalty, www.sisterhelen.org

Texas Defender Service: www.texasdefender.org

The National Registry of Exonerations, www.law.umich.edu/special/exoneration/Pages/about.aspx

Witness to Innocence, www.witnesstoinnocence.org

Books and Articles:

Balko, Radley, "Transcript Reveals Shocking Grand Jury Intimidation of Witnesses," *The Washington Post*, July 17, 2014.

Balko, Radley, "Houston Grand Juries: Too White, Too Law-and-Order, and Too Cozy with Cops," *The Washington Post*, August 1, 2014.

Balko, Radley, "Exclusive: Houston Cop Who Threatened, Harassed Grand Jury Witness Served on at Least Nine Other Grand Juries," *The Washington Post*, August 8, 2014.

Basu, Moni, "Dead Man Walking Nun: Botched Executions Unmask a Botched System," *CNN.com*, August 6, 2014.

Bier, Daniel, "Scalia's Defense of the Death Penalty is in Tatters," *Newsweek.com*, June 14, 2015.

Berkowitz, Bonnie, Keating, Dan, and Johnson, Richard, "An Eye for an Eye?," *The Washington Post*, May 18, 2014.

Colloff, Pamela, "Innocence Lost," *Texas Monthly*, October 2010.

Dallas Morning News Editorial, "Another Big Reason to Rethink Capital Punishment," June 14, 2016.

Death Penalty Information Center, "Georgia Sets Execution Date Despite Unanimous Findings of Mental Retardation and Pending Supreme Court Review," July 8, 2013.

Dershowitz, Alan M., "Scalia's Catholic Betrayal," *The Daily Beast*, August 18, 2009.

Diamond, Jeremy, "Bill Clinton Concedes Role in Mass Incarceration," *CNN.com*, May 7, 2015.

Early, Mark L, "A Pink Cadillac, an IQ of 63, and a Fourteen-Year-Old from South Carolina: Why I can No Longer Support The Death Penalty," *University of Richmond Law Review*, Vol. 49:811, March 13, 2015.

Egelko, Bob, "Death Row Isn't a High-Income Neighborhood, Nation's Legal Experts Say," *Los Angeles Times*, September 11, 1994.

Ergun, Damla, "New Low in Preference for the Death Penalty," *ABC News*, June 5, 2014.

Falkenberg, Lisa, Houston Chronicle Article Series: www.houstonchronicle.com/local/dead-man-waiting/

Falkenberg, Lisa, "Does 'Pick-a-Pal' System Give you a Grand Jury of your Peers?" August 13, 2014.

Falkenberg, Lisa, "Appeals Court Resets Murder Trial After Finding Evidence Withheld," *Houston Chronicle*, November 5, 2014.

Falkenberg, Lisa, "DA's Probe of Former Death Row Inmate Raises Concerns," *Houston Chronicle*, April 18, 2015.

Flood, Mary and Rogers, Brian, "Election Defeat Stuns Incumbent Harris County Judges," *Houston Chronicle*, November 6, 2008.

Grisham, John, "The Innocent Man: Murder and Injustice in a Small Town," *Dell* 2012.

Grissom, Brandi, "Psychologist Who Cleared Death Row Inmates is Reprimanded," *The New York Times*, April 14, 2011.

Gross, Samuel, et. al., "Rate of False Conviction of Criminal Defendants Who are Sentenced to Death," 111 No. 20, *Proceedings of the National Academy of Sciences* (2014).

Hooper, Don, "Harris County Grand Jury System Needs Reform, Patricia Pollard: An Example of a System Gone Wrong," *Big Jolly Politics*, August 15, 2014.

Houston Chronicle Editorial, "Grand Juries: Potential Jurors Should be Picked from a Random Pool Taken from Public Records," August 22, 2014.

Houston Chronicle Editorial, "Chronicle's Falkenberg Wins Pulitzer for Commentary," April 20, 2015.

Houston Chronicle Editorial Board, "An Innocent Man," June 10, 2015.

Itkowitz, Colby, "For Lawyer, a Friendship Forged on Death Row," *The Washington Post*, January 25, 2016.

Jervis, Rick, "Texas Soon to Hit Grim Milestone: 500th Execution," *USA Today*, June 25, 2013.

Johnson, Carrie, "Report: Prosecutors Hid Evidence in Ted Stevens Case," *NPR.org*, March 15, 2012.

Knafo, Saki, "1 in 3 Black Males Will Go to Prison in Their Lifetime, Report Warns," *Huffington Post*, October 4, 2013.

Kozinski, Alex (Hon.), "Criminal Law 2.0," *Georgetown Law Journal Annual Review of Criminal Procedure*, Vol. 44 (2015).

Levine, Dan, and Cooke, Christina, "Uneven Justice -- In states with elected high court judges, a harder line on capital punishment," *Reuters Investigates*, September 22, 2015.

Lewis, Anthony, Gideon's Trumpet, *Vintage*, 1964.

Lewis, Neil, "Tables Turned on Prosecution in Stevens Case," *New York Times*, April 7, 2009.

Lezon, Dale, "Convicted Killer Proclaims his Innocence to Jury; Outburst Occurs as Prosecutor Argues for the Death Penalty," *Houston Chronicle*, October 25, 2005.

Lozano, Juan, "Unusual Grand Jury System Used Only in Texas is Reassesed Because of Bias Concerns, Associated Press, March 17, 2015.

Lussenhop, Jessica, "Why Harris County, Texas Leads the US in Exonerations," *BBC News*, February 12, 2016.

Marazziti, Mario, and Elie, Paul, "13 Ways of Looking at the Death Penalty," *Seven Stories Press*, 2015.

Marlowe, Jen, Martina Correia-Davis, "I am Troy Davis," *Haymarket Books*, 2013.

Mauro, Tony, "Gideon remains 'a wake-up call'," *National Law Journal*, March 18, 2013.

Millhiser, Ian, "Scalia says there's nothing unconstitutional about executing the innocent," *Thinkprogress.org*, August 17, 2009.

McDonough, Molly, "Psychologist's Reprimand Gives Hope to Counsel for Death Row Inmates," *American Bar Association*, April 15, 2011.

McVicker, Steve, "Study: Police Ties Common in Grand Juries," *Houston Chronicle*. November 14, 2014.

New York Times Editorial Board, "Rampant Prosecutorial Misconduct," January 4, 2014.

Nicholson, Eric, "Texas Falls Out of Love With the Death Penalty, Embraces Life Without Parole," *Dallas Observer*, December 17, 2015.

O'Hare, Peggy, "Man Sentenced to Death in Officer's Killing," *Houston Chronicle*, October 26, 2005.

Perry, Rick, "Black Lives Matter - And So Does Black Liberty," Forbes.com, July 27, 2016.

Prejean, Sister Helen, "Dead Man Walking: The Eyewitness Account Of The Death Penalty That Sparked a National Debate," *Vintage*, 1994.

Prejean, Sister Helen, "The Death of Innocents, An Eyewitness Account of Wrongful Executions," *Vintage*, 2005.

Ridgeway, James, and Casella, Jean. "America's 10 Worst Prisons: Polunsky – The Hardest Place to do Time in Texas – and Then You Die," *Mother Jones*, May 2, 2013.

Rogers, Brian, "Widow of Mike Anderson Appointed New Harris County District Attorney," *Houston Chronicle*, September 24, 2013.

Rogers, Brian, "Appeals Court tosses capital murder conviction in death of HPD officer," *Houston Chronicle*, November 5, 2014.

Rogers, Brian, "Houston Lawyers Group Urges Probe of Ex-Prosecutor," *Houston Chronicle*, November 18, 2014.

Rogers, Brian, "DA Drops Murder Charge in Killing of HPD Officer," *Houston Chronicle*, June 9, 2015.

Ruiz, Rosana and Tolson, Mike, "Capital Punishment on Decline in County," *Houston Chronicle*, July 25, 2007.

Sapien, Joaquin and Hernandez, Sergio, "Who Polices Prosecutors Who Abuse Their Authority? Usually Nobody," *ProPublica.org*, April 3, 2013.

Savage, Charlie, "Prosecutors Face Penalty in '08 Trial of a Senator," *New York Times*, May 24, 2012.

Schieber, Vicki, et. al. "Where Justice and Mercy Meet," *Catholic Mobilizing Network*, Liturgical Press, 2013.

Solomon, Dan, "Is the Grand Jury System in Texas Broken?" *Texas Monthly*, July 30, 2014.

Sutton, Joe, "Maryland Governor Signs Death Penalty Repeal," *CNN.com*, May 2, 2013.

Texas Defender Service, "Toward More Transparent Justice: The Michael Morton Act's First Year," 2015.

The Sentencing Project, "Report of The Sentencing Project to the United Nations Human Rights Committee," August 2013.

Turow, Scott, "Ultimate Punishment, A Lawyer's Reflection on Dealing with the Death Penalty," Farrar, Straus and Giroux, 2003.

US Courts.gov, "Criminal Justice Act: At 50 Years, a Landmark in the Right to Counsel," August 20, 2014.

Walsh, Mark, "Fifty years after Gideon, lawyers still struggle to provide counsel to the indigent," *ABA Journal*, March 1, 2013.

Washington Post, Obituaries, "Freed After Years on Death Row," July 5, 2015.

Wheaton, Sarah, "Obama Commutes 214 sentences," *Politico*, August 3, 2016.

Wisk, Allison, "Death Knell for 'Pick-a-Pal' Grand Juror Selection in Texas as Overhaul Bill Heads to Abbott," *Dallas Morning News*, May 31, 2015.

Index